Nick Spencer is Director of Studies at Theos, the public theology think tank. He is the author of a number of books and reports, most recently 'Neither Private nor Privileged: The Role of Christianity in Britain Today' (Theos, 2007).

DARWIN AND GOD

Nick Spencer

First published in Great Britain in 2009

Society for Promoting Christian Knowledge
36 Causton Street
London SW1P 4ST

British Library Cataloguing-in-Publication Data
A catalogue record for this book is available from the British Library

ISBN 978–0–281–06082–5

1 3 5 7 9 10 8 6 4 2

Typeset by Graphicraft Limited, Hong Kong
Printed in Great Britain by Ashford Colour Press

Produced on paper from sustainable forests

Contents

Acknowledgements

————◆◆◆————

I am hugely grateful to a number of people who have helped improve this book. My colleagues Paul Woolley and Paul Bickley read the original manuscript carefully and offered valuable comments. Jennie Pollock not only gave similarly helpful comments but also did a superb job of weeding out the innumerable small errors that had crept into the text.

Denis Alexander, Ian Christie and John Hedley Brooke each took time to read and comment on the first draft, for which I am particularly grateful, given their busy schedules.

Darwin and God is part of a larger project undertaken by Theos, the public theology think tank, and the Faraday Institute for Science and Religion, which was made possible by a generous grant from The Templeton Foundation, for which I am deeply thankful.

I owe a debt of gratitude also to SPCK, who caught the idea for a book on Darwin's religious beliefs straight away, and to Alison Barr, who offered her usual perceptive comments in the editing process.

My greatest debt of thanks is, of course, to Kate, my wife, and to Ellen and Jonny, my children.

Last, but certainly not least, Toby Hole took the time to read *Darwin and God*, as he has every book I have written. His comments were as incisive and encouraging as his example of Christian faith and intellectual rigour has been inspiring to me. It is with great pleasure that I dedicate this book to him.

Nick Spencer
London, Autumn 2008

Timeline

1809   Born on 12 February in Shrewsbury, son of Robert Waring and Susannah Darwin, née Wedgwood

1817   Starts at school run by Unitarian minister, George Case; mother dies

1818–25   Attends Shrewsbury School as a boarder

1825–7   Studies medicine at Edinburgh University, initially with his brother, Erasmus

1827   Leaves Edinburgh; father encourages him to ordination in the Church of England; admitted to Christ's College, Cambridge, but does not take up residence until January 1828

1828–31   Studies (and collects insects) at Cambridge; passes BA in January 1831; remains for a further two terms to fulfil residence requirement

1831   Name put forward as a potential companion for Captain FitzRoy on *Beagle* voyage to survey South American coast

1831–6   Travels on *Beagle*

1836–7   Returns to Shrewsbury, then Cambridge and London; starts publishing scientific papers

1837–9   Begins speculating on species evolution in private notebooks that form the basis of his theory; discusses his religious scepticism with future wife, Emma

1839   Marries Emma on 29 January; first child, William, born; publishes *Voyage of the Beagle*

1841   Daughter Anne (Annie) born

Timeline

1842	Moves to Down House, Downe, Kent; makes initial sketch of his species theory
1844	Writes second, longer species sketch
1846–54	Works on barnacles; sporadic illnesses intensify
1848	Father dies
1849	Tries water treatment for his illness in Malvern
1851	Takes Annie to Malvern for water treatment. She falls ill and dies on 23 April, aged ten
1854	Completes barnacles work and returns to work on species theory
1856–7	Begins writing up theory into a projected big book called 'Natural Selection'
1858	Receives a letter from Alfred Russel Wallace that contains an identical theory of evolution; persuaded to co-present Wallace's paper and one of his own at Linnean Society on 1 July (although he is absent from meeting); begins 'abstract' of his long species book, which becomes *The Origin of Species*
1859	*The Origin of Species* published on 24 November; second edition follows in months
1860–2	Works on orchids
1863–6	Serious and prolonged bouts of ill-health
1868	Publishes *The Variation of Animals and Plants Under Domestication*
1871	Publishes *The Descent of Man*
1872	Publishes *The Expression of the Emotions in Man and Animals*
1876	Begins to write an autobiographical memoir
1882	Dies 19 April, aged 73; buried a week later in Westminster Abbey

Introduction

Charles Darwin died an agnostic. He disliked theological speculation. He believed one could be both 'an ardent theist & an
evolutionist'.[1] And he hated religious controversy. 'Why should
you be so aggressive?' he asked the atheist Edward Aveling in
1881. 'Is anything gained by trying to force these new ideas upon
the mass of mankind?'[2]

Somehow, in spite of this, recent years have seen Darwin
adopted as the icon of thinking atheism. His theory of evolution by natural selection supposedly makes disbelief in God
'intellectually fulfilling' and sends all other explanations of
life, purpose and meaning to the philosophical dustbin. In
the words of one such Darwinian, 'When you are actually challenged to think of pre-Darwinian answers to the questions
"What is man?" "Is there a meaning to life?" "What are we for?"
can you . . . think of any that are not now worthless?'[3]

Religious believers who turn to Darwin for succour are
unlikely to find him any more comforting, however. Darwin had
a Christian faith and he lost it. In spite of rumours to the
contrary, he did not convert to Christianity or renounce
evolution on his deathbed. He did not believe in the divinity
of Jesus Christ or in the possibility of revelation. He may have
been buried in the nave of Westminster Abbey, yards away
from the missionary David Livingstone, but he shared precious
little of Livingstone's orthodox Christian faith.

It is precisely this that makes him such an interesting figure.
In spite of efforts to prove otherwise, Darwin is too subtle, too
thoughtful, too interesting a figure to manipulate. As the academic John Hedley Brooke has commented, we need to be very

careful about trying to pigeon-hole the man who wouldn't pigeon-hole pigeons.[4]

A play in three acts

For a man who eschewed religious controversy, Darwin has probably had more impact on religious thinking than anyone else born in the last 200 years. The literature on Darwinism and religion or Darwinism and Christianity or Darwinism and God is enormous. From those who claim the former disproves the latter, to those who claim the latter disproves the former, through many shades of accommodation in between, everyone has something to say on the subject.

It is somewhat strange, then, that so little has been written on the topic of Darwin's own religious beliefs. At the time of writing, there is one short book, published six years ago in the USA, and a handful of academic articles, most of which were out of print or simply inaccessible to the general reader.

This book aims to fill that gap by charting Darwin's religious journey. The publication of his Complete Works online (<darwin-online.org.uk>) has provided a wealth of useful material for such a project, as has the coming online of Darwin's voluminous correspondence in the Darwin Correspondence Project (<darwinproject.ac.uk>). These sources have enabled easy access to those opinions that Darwin was careful to keep out of print in his lifetime.

When Darwin was in his late twenties his father had warned him to keep religious doubts to himself. Thirty-five years later, he gave the same advice to his son George. Darwin was not a man to wear his personal beliefs, of any kind, on his sleeve, and was not living in an age in which such candour was encouraged.

In spite of this, and occasional protestations to the contrary, he clearly thought deeply about religious matters and was prepared to disclose his opinions to family, close friends and even, towards the end of his life, strangers who wrote to him for his views on the subject. His opinions were rarely spelled out at length and never articulated systematically but they are there, to be pieced together.

What emerges from the jigsaw are three relatively clear stages in his journey – the period until his return from the *Beagle* voyage in 1836, the period between then and the death of his daughter Annie in 1851, and the period thereafter. During the first of these Darwin was clearly a Christian but, as we shall see, a Christian of a particular kind, a kind that prepared the ground for his subsequent loss of faith. This period is covered in Chapter 1.

The Charles Darwin who returned from the *Beagle* in 1836 may not have been as orthodox as the one who left nearly five years earlier – the thought of becoming a clergyman, the dreadful fate from which the *Beagle* saved him, was now absurd – but he was still a Christian believer of sorts. The 15 years or so between his return and Annie's death constitute the crucial period during which his Christian faith was extinguished. Chapter 2 explores these years, arguing that although his autobiography suggests that a number of intellectual doubts conspired to kill his faith, it was the problem of suffering – at first theoretically and then personally – that wielded the knife.

Darwin's religious journey did not end in 1851. He latterly described himself as a 'theist' while writing *The Origin of Species* in the late 1850s, although his theism appears to have rejected the possibility of revelation or God's interaction with the world and was, in reality, closer to deism, the belief in a God who created the universe and then withdrew into silent indifference.

Darwin only began to doubt the grounds for his belief in a creator towards the end of his life. This was a period of both candour and confusion. He wrote more openly about his religious convictions in the 1860s and 1870s than at any previous time, despite being less sure of them. There was a sense that, after Annie's death, it no longer mattered so much. Ultimately he was happiest with the label agnostic, a word coined by his friend Thomas Huxley. Chapter 3 explores this concluding period.

The final chapter looks briefly at what we can learn from Darwin's religious journey. The issues that he explored in his lifetime remain live ones. What constitutes appropriate evidence for religious belief? How far is 'nature' a valid foundation for religious belief? Are there signs of design or purpose within creation? Is religious experience important? Is the idea of divine revelation credible? What is the legitimate level of proof one can demand? How far can we trust our own minds in such matters? And, of course, how can suffering be reconciled with God? Such questions remain as meaningful to millions today as they were in 1859.

Chapter 4 also reminds us that there is as much to learn from the *way* in which Darwin engaged with such questions as there is from the questions themselves. Indeed, in the current intellectual climate, Darwin's manner of engagement stands out as especially relevant.

Given the anger and vitriol that have been vented in what have been called the 'Darwin Wars', it is a pleasure to read Darwin's own musings on the matter. Hesitant, respectful, self-critical and disarmingly self-deprecatory, Darwin's thinking exhibits all the qualities that seem absent from the 'debate' today.

'I hardly see how religion & science can be kept . . . distinct,' he once wrote to J. Brodie Innes, the vicar of Downe with whom he shared a lifelong friendship. 'But . . . there is no reason why the disciples of either school should attack each other with bitterness.'[5]

1

'A sort of Christian':
the faith Darwin lost

The great majority of naturalists believe that species are
immutable productions, and have been separately created ...
Some few naturalists, on the other hand, believe that species
undergo modification, and that the existing forms of life have
descended by true generation from preexisting forms.[6]

It is often remarked that evolution was in the air in the early
nineteenth century. Darwin himself, although always keen to
emphasize his own originality, began the third edition of *The
Origin of Species* with a 'historical sketch' of those 'few naturalists' who were evolutionists before him. He mentioned,
among others, Jean-Baptiste Lamarck ('the first man whose
conclusions on this subject excited much attention'), Geoffroy
Saint-Hilaire, the Revd William Herbert and Robert Grant, a
friend of Darwin's while at Edinburgh, all of whom had published evolutionary ideas before Darwin developed his own in
the 1830s.

Darwin had little to lose from such candour. His own
theory was significantly different from those of his predeces-
sors – his evolution was *by natural selection* – and it, unlike theirs,
was supported by a mountain of careful and detailed observation. Nevertheless, it is fair to say that evolution was a theory
waiting to happen. It was, in the words of Darwin's friend Charles
Lyell, hanging tensely in the air.

Much the same could be said for Darwin's loss of Christian faith. Darwin was born into a Christian family deeply

embedded within a Christian culture. But the *kind* of Christianity in which he grew up prepared the way for its subsequent disappearance in his life. As with evolution, the story begins before Darwin's birth, this time more than a century before.

When the first defences of Christianity were written in the early seventeenth century, against sceptics, deists and as yet invisible atheists, they were works of philosophy. Early apologists wrote as philosophers, despite usually being theologians. Battles were fought on territory judged to be open and accessible to everyone, in particular the territory of nature.

Nature was, in Sir Thomas Browne's words, a 'universal and public manuscript'.[7] Unlike biblical revelation or personal experience, it did not depend on confessional allegiances or unverifiable testimony. The glories of the heavens, the splendour of the earth, the complexity of the human body – all were open for all to see. The ground was laid for theological debates that were not really theological but, instead, based primarily on philosophical arguments from existence, design, complexity or universal religiosity.

As Europe endured the slaughter of a 30-year war that was, in large measure, a religious affair, it became more hostile to arguments that relied on ecclesiastical structure or sacred texts. In the words of the historian Michael Buckley, 'the Western conscience found itself deeply scandalized and disgusted by confessional religions . . . Religious warfare irrevocably discredited confessional primacy in the growing secularized sensitivity of much European culture.'[8]

As a result, the philosophical turn instituted earlier in the seventeenth century grew in popularity. Nature revealed an order and benignity from which a truly universal and harmonious conception of God might be derived. Neither experience nor revelation, either in textual or ecclesiastical format, was necessary as a means of establishing the truths of the Christian religion. God's 'book of works' was enough.

When this natural theology first emerged as a powerful force in England in the seventeenth century, it did so as one device among many, wielded alongside more conventional appeals to scripture, ecclesiastical authority and even personal experience. However, as the eighteenth century progressed, it moved from being the supporting act to the headlining one.

There were problems. Such natural theology did not, it emerged, point towards the *Christian* religion but rather to a kind of deism, in which God was understood as the supreme example of what civilized Westerners understood to be good, just and wise. His role was reduced to that of a first cause, with little relevance thereafter. Nonetheless, the arguments remained popular, reaching their apogee at the turn of the nineteenth century in the work of William Paley, Archdeacon of Carlisle.

Paley was the most influential British theologian at the time of Darwin's birth. His *Principles of Moral and Political Philosophy* (1785) and *Evidences of Christianity* (1794) were compulsory texts for those who wished to be ordained into the established Church. However, it is for his *Natural Theology; or Evidences of the Existence and Attributes of the Deity, Collected from their Appearances in Nature*, published in 1802, that he is most famous.

Paley transposed the arguments from physical design, which had proved so popular in the seventeenth and early eighteenth centuries, into arguments from biological design. Nature, he argued, contains 'every indication of contrivance, every manifestation of design'. His *Natural Theology* proceeded to examine a great many of these 'manifestations', in plants, animals and humans, all the time arguing that such 'contrivances' could not be accident but were, rather, an indication of the direct work of a Deity, whose unity, personality and goodness Paley went on to explore. 'Design must have had a designer,' he reasoned. 'That designer must have been a person. That person is God.'[9]

Paley's work proved enormously popular and influential, not simply because it appeared irrefutable but also because its publication coincided with the Napoleonic era. *Natural Theology* offered a vision of security and stability that the nation and, in particular, the governing class, craved.[10] Accordingly, Paleyian natural theology and its assumptions found their way into Church, universities and society as a whole, serving the dual function of demonstrating the existence of a benign and ordered deity, and protecting society against threats of social and political revolution. Christianity underpinned social order and Paleyian theology underpinned Christianity.

It was this intellectual climate that formed the basis of the part-Anglican, part-Unitarian culture into which Charles Robert Darwin was born, in Shrewsbury, on 12 February 1809. His family background, on both sides, was illustrious and vaguely unconventional. His grandfather on his mother's side was Josiah Wedgwood, whose high-quality pottery and commercial intelligence propelled the family into high society. He was a Unitarian, believing in God but rejecting the doctrines of the Trinity, incarnation, Fall, atonement and revelation. Unitarianism, Darwin's other grandfather teased, was merely 'a featherbed to catch a falling Christian'.

That grandfather, Erasmus Darwin, made Josiah Wedgwood look positively orthodox. Born in 1731, he was a man of his age: a disciple of the notorious French *philosophes*, a prophet of progress and poet of liberty, evolutionist, freethinker, rationalist, and disposed towards materialism and atheism if not quite advocating either. For him science replaced religion. His poems worshipped at the altar of Nature and suggested (vaguely) that life did not need a creator but arose 'without parent by spontaneous birth', thereafter advancing of its own volition, governed only by the laws of nature.[11]

Grandfather Erasmus was an assertive and opinionated man, and although he died seven years before Charles' birth, his influence on the family and his grandson remained considerable. Darwin wrote in his autobiography that he 'admired greatly' Erasmus' biological work, *Zoönomia*, although, ever keen to downplay any intellectual debts, he went on to say that 'on reading it a second time . . . I was much disappointed, the proportion of speculation being so large to the facts given.'[12]

These freethinking and Unitarian influences on Darwin blended with more conventional ones. His grandparents and parents were wealthy, entrepreneurial Whigs, who had no interest in political revolution. His father, Robert Waring Darwin, was a country doctor and, for 50 years, the most significant financier in the region. Anti-Tory and vehemently critical of aristocracy and privilege, he had little religious faith himself. Darwin described him as a 'free thinker in religious matters' with only 'nominal' attachment to the Church of England. He was, in the words of one biographer, 'probably an atheist', once remarking to Darwin that although there were 'only the vaguest hints' that his sister-in-law, Kitty Wedgwood, was herself an atheist, he felt that 'so clear-sighted a woman could not be a believer'.[13]

Darwin himself was tutored briefly by a Unitarian minister, the Reverend George Case, whose chapel meetings his mother attended. When he was eight, however, his mother died and Darwin was taken back home. Her death might have devastated him but seems to have had little lasting impact. 'I can remember hardly anything about her,' he wrote in his autobiography 60 years later, going on to explain that 'my forgetfulness is partly due to my sisters, owing to their great grief, never being able to speak about her or mention her name'.[14] Following her death, his sister Caroline took it upon herself to continue his education, teaching him his Bible and moving him from the Unitarian chapel to the parish church, at which he had been christened.

A year later, at the age of nine, Darwin was sent to the local school. He boarded, with his older brother Erasmus, despite the school being less than a mile from home. Shrewsbury school was typical of its age, immersing the sons of local landowners in the classics before sending them off to Oxford or Cambridge. Darwin remained there until he was 16, benefiting little from his education. 'Nothing could have been worse for the development of my mind than Dr. Butler's school,' he recalled. The curriculum was 'strictly classical' with 'much attention paid to learning by heart the lessons of the previous day'.[15] It did nothing to encourage his interest in nature, collecting and experimentation, which was already becoming an obsession.

Erasmus left for Cambridge to study medicine in 1822, moving to Edinburgh three years later, in order to attend an authorized medical school and fulfil the requirements of his degree. Darwin was clearly not flourishing at school, even less now that his brother had left, so his father decided to send him to Edinburgh. Darwin later claimed that his and Erasmus' 'minds and tastes were . . . so different that I do not think that I owe much to him intellectually'.[16] That may have been so, but leaving Shrewsbury for Edinburgh was a cause for much celebration. Erasmus' company was stimulating, and although Darwin never took to medicine, Edinburgh removed him from an atmosphere of stultifying classicism and brought him a little closer to real science.

Edinburgh

Edinburgh in the 1820s was everything Shrewsbury wasn't: heterodox, cosmopolitan, intellectually vigorous. It may have been the home of Scotland's ecclesiastical establishment, but it was also subversive, even radical, having long been a haven for dissenters barred from Oxbridge.

Medicine in Edinburgh was divided between official lectures and unofficial or 'extramural' ones. The official ones tended towards the theoretical, inhabiting the natural theology tradition and articulating a harmonious vision of the physical (and socio-political) order. The extramural classes were more practical, encouraging hands-on experience through experimentation, dissection and surgery.

They were also more radical. Drawing on Continental thought, they taught a form of comparative anatomy 'which endeavoured to understand the structure and function of living beings without reference to any obvious divine causes'.[17] Although not outrightly atheistic, the goal of such education was not to show how the intricate workings of the body pointed towards a just and good creator so much as to show how life itself could have emerged out of organization alone. God, spirit and soul were notable for their absence.

Darwin chose the more conservative option and did not attend any extramural classes. That did not make medicine more attractive, however. He found most classes dull and the practical work he observed repelled him. 'I attended on two occasions the operating theatre in the hospital at Edinburgh, and saw two very bad operations, one on a child, but I rushed away before they were completed,' he confessed in his autobiography. 'Hardly any inducement' could have persuaded him to return, 'this being long before the blessed days of chloroform. The two cases fairly haunted me for many a long year.'[18]

Edinburgh did not turn Darwin into an atheist or materialist or even a sceptic, but it did immerse him in a culture in which these beliefs were intellectually possible. Darwin was familiar with men like Robert Grant, Robert Knox and William Browne, anti-clerical freethinkers whose science and scepticism scandalized the authorities. According to a notorious paper Browne delivered to the Plinian society in March 1827 (at which Darwin delivered his first scientific paper), mind and consciousness were not spiritual entities, separate from the body, but simply spin-offs from brain activity. According to Grant, who worshipped the French evolutionists Lamarck and Saint-Hilaire, all life was related, having evolved from the simplest algae. Darwin became one of Grant's walking companions, pacing the coast around Edinburgh, searching for shore life and talking about evolution.

Such talk was dangerous. Evolution, or transmutation as it was more commonly known, was condemned by both ecclesiastical and scientific authorities (usually, of course, the same thing). It was profoundly subversive, threatening to undermine the foundations of society with its talk of change and self-development. The order of things was guaranteed by God and secured by his authorities on earth. If that order were mutable, moreover if it were mutable in such a way as to allow 'lower' life-forms to turn into 'higher' ones, everything could fall apart. One only had to look at the savagery and tyranny of revolutionary and post-revolutionary France, where such doctrines had held more sway, to see where such thinking led.[19]

This association of evolution with atheism and radicalism made a deep impression on Darwin, one that was to shape the course of his whole life. At the time, however, it did not appear to have a significant impact on him or on his conventional religiosity, although that seems, from the brief glimpse we have of it, to have been lukewarm at best.

His sister Caroline wrote to him in March 1826, with news of home life, and a brief admonition. 'Dear Charles I hope you read the bible', she said, '& not only because you think it wrong not to read it, but with the wish of learning there what is necessary to feel & do to go to heaven after you die.' 'I suppose you do not feel prepared yet to take the sacrament,' she asked tentatively.[20]

Darwin replied the following month, dutifully saying that he had 'tried to follow your advice about the Bible', and going on to ask 'what part of [it] do you like best?' 'I like the Gospels,' he declared. 'Do you know which of them is generally reckoned the best?'[21]

A few days later Caroline replied with more family news, again encouraging him over such 'grave matters'. She was 'glad' that he had been 'studying the bible', agreeing that 'St John [is] the best of the Gospels'. She then confided that she 'often regret[s] myself that when I was younger & fuller of pursuits & high spirits I was not more religious – but it is very difficult to be so habitually'.[22]

It is a brief but telling exchange, not least coming from the pen of a man shortly to train for the Anglican ministry. However orthodox Darwin's faith might have been, in terms of giving assent to the right things, he appeared to lack motivation. Caroline needed gently to encourage him, and although he responded correctly, there was clearly little deeply felt, personal conviction. Years later, Darwin would write as an aside in his autobiography, 'I do not think that the religious sentiment was ever strongly developed in me.'[23] His sister seemed to recognize this.

Cambridge

Erasmus left Edinburgh in 1826 and Charles the following year. The northern capital had done little for his interest in medicine, although it had nurtured his passion for science and nature. It had also seen him develop his taste for shooting and other country sports. Darwin was in danger of becoming an 'idle sporting man', according to his frustrated father. Recognizing that his son was not cut out to follow him into medicine, he proposed ordination.

Some people are surprised when they first learn that the supposed architect of scientific atheism was once destined for the priesthood. Darwin himself commented on the irony in his autobiography, remarking that 'considering how fiercely I have been attacked by the orthodox it seems ludicrous that I once intended to be a clergyman'.[24] Those who express surprise, however, tend to be unaware that ordination, at least into the established Church of the time, was not necessarily the most spiritual of vocations.

When, a few years later, Darwin's uncle, Josiah Wedgwood, was trying to persuade his father to allow Darwin to travel on the *Beagle*, he reasoned that not only would such a journey not be 'in any degree disreputable to his character as a Clergyman', but that 'the pursuit of Natural History' was in fact 'very suitable to a clergyman'.[25] Becoming an Anglican vicar in the early nineteenth century did not necessarily testify to a deep-felt spiritual calling, still less a Damascene conversion. In the words of Adrian Desmond and James Moore, the Anglican Church of the time was 'fat, complacent, and corrupt, liv[ing] luxuriously on its tithes and endowments, as it had for a century'.[26] Wealthy livings were regularly auctioned to the highest bidder, and clergymen enjoyed a life of status, comfort and leisure. If Darwin agreed to ordination, 'he would be set up for life . . . enjoy[ing] social prominence, a steady income, and eventually a handsome legacy'.[27] A serious personal belief in God was no bar to the Anglican ministry – Darwin's good friend John Stevens Henslow managed to combine scientific eminence and genuine piety as rector of Hitcham in Suffolk – but nor was it a necessity.

To his credit, Darwin paused. In his autobiography he recorded how 'I asked for some time to consider [my father's offer].'[28] There was much that appealed in the life of a country clergyman but Darwin knew that his personal convictions were weak. 'From what little I had heard and thought on the subject,' he relates in his autobiography, 'I had scruples about declaring my belief in all the dogmas of the Church of England.'[29] His hesitation is testimony to his integrity. How he dealt with it is testimony to the nature of the Christianity he was expected to profess.

He read some books. Specifically, he read Bishop John Pearson's *Exposition of the Creed*, and 'a few other books on divinity', including *The Evidence of Christianity derived from its Nature and Reception* by the Revd John Bird Sumner, published in 1821.

Pearson's book had proved popular and influential when first published, but since that was 1659 it was a little out of date by the time Darwin got to it. The book was a careful, article-by-article examination of the Apostles' Creed. He set out his method in an introductory note 'To the reader'.

> This therefore is the method which I . . . have prosecuted in every Article. First, to settle the words of each Article according to their antiquity and generality of reception in the Creed. Secondly, to explicate and unfold the terms, and to endeavour a right notion and conception of them as they are to be understood in the same. Thirdly, to shew what are those truths which are naturally contained in those terms so explicated, and to make it appear that they are truths indeed, by such arguments and reasons as are respectively proper to evidence the verity of them. Fourthly, to declare what is the necessity of believing those truths, what efficacy and influence they have in the soul, and upon the life of a believer. Lastly, by a recollection of all, briefly to deliver the sum of every particular truth, so that every one, when he pronounceth the Creed, may know what he ought to intend, and what he is understood to profess, when he so pronounceth it.[30]

Darwin read the book 'with care'.

Sumner, later to become Archbishop of Canterbury, was more engaging. He claimed that, 'though there is just cause for believing that real religion never flourished more in any age or country than at the present time in Britain . . . it is certain that a vast number of persons reject it, either avowedly or virtually'.[31] His *Evidence* was intended to rectify this woeful state of affairs, 'illustrat[ing] . . . that a religion like the Christian could never have existed, unless it had been introduced by divine authority'.[32] Citing evidence, applying logic and establishing conclusions, Sumner demonstrated that

> whether we consider the doctrines introduced by its Author . . . or . . . the internal evidence of the Christian writings . . . or . . . the peculiar character formed under the influence of

Christianity ... or ... the rapidity with which a religion so pure, so self-denying, so humiliating, and so uncompromising was propagated and embraced, even in the face of bitter hostility: – we have phenomena which nothing, except the truth of the religion, can adequately explain.[33]

Darwin was impressed. 'I did not then in the least doubt the strict and literal truth of every word in the Bible [and] soon persuaded myself that our Creed must be fully accepted.'[34]

Pearson and Sumner offer a good indication of the neat, rational, orthodox Christianity to which Darwin adhered in his pre-*Beagle* days. Not so much a personal commitment to the person and work of Christ, still less an affecting encounter with the Holy Spirit, this Christianity was a series of propositions to be accepted, a hypothesis to be satisfactorily established, an argument to be won.

Duly convinced, Darwin entered Christ's College in January 1828. Cambridge at the time was a microcosm of early nineteenth-century Britain, 'if not a society of Christians, [it] was at least regarded as a Christian society'.[35] Founded on, structured and governed by the strictures of Anglican Christianity, it was thoroughly orthodox and thoroughly establishment. Only those who declared their belief in the thirty-nine Articles could take a degree. Students were compelled to study theology and moral philosophy; fellows to take Holy Orders. Masters and fellows were leading national figures, holding, with Oxford, the right of patronage for many desirable parishes. Attendance at daily chapel services was compulsory, although scarcely more that a pre-dinner formality. As John Stuart Mill later remarked, 'No thought can find place [there] except that which can reconcile itself with orthodoxy.'[36]

Darwin settled in well, making some close and influential friends, and taking to a life of shooting, walking, gambling, drinking, eating and collecting beetles. When he arrived in 1828 no rooms were available in his college, so he took lodgings nearby until the following October. By an appealing quirk of fate, the rooms he took had once been occupied by William Paley.

Paley impressed Darwin. He was required to study his *Principles of Moral and Political Philosophy* and *View of the Evidences of Christianity* as part of his degree, and remarked, 'I am convinced that I could have written out the whole of the *Evidences* with perfect correctness, but not of course in the clear language of Paley.'[37] He also read, by choice, and delighted in, Paley's *Natural Theology*, commenting in his autobiography that it 'gave me as much delight as did Euclid'.[38]

Darwin was required to translate certain prescribed classical texts, together with portions of the Gospels and the Acts of the Apostles, for his 'Little Go' examinations in March 1830, but it was Paley's arguments that really energized him. In reality, Paley was already falling out of favour by 1830, criticized for 'his emphasis on Bentham's utilitarian principles' by fellows who sought to remove him from students' compulsory reading lists.[39] His *Principles of Moral and Political Philosophy* was increasingly recognized as outdated and, crucially, not especially Christian. Paley 'based his notions of right and wrong on purely natural reasoning, confident that all men could be brought to agree'.[40] That might have been so 50 years earlier, but the world had changed since then.

His *Natural Theology* faced similar problems. His was a vision of natural order and goodness that owed rather more to the comfortable, established lifestyle of its author and the society in which he moved, than to the New Testament. Paley's was 'a happy world' teeming with 'delighted existence'. 'In a spring noon, or a summer evening,' he remarked, 'on whichever side I turn my eyes, myriads of happy beings crowd upon my view.'[41]

Such a view was hardly ubiquitous, even among leading Christians. Some years before *Natural Theology* was published John Wesley, following St Paul, had observed in a sermon on 'The General Deliverance':

How true then is that word, 'God saw everything that he had made: and behold it was very good!' But how far is this from being the present case! In what a condition is the whole lower world! – to say nothing of inanimate nature, wherein all the elements seem to be out of course, and by turns to fight against man. Since man rebelled against his Maker, in what a state is all animated nature! Well might the Apostle say of this: 'The whole creation groaneth and travaileth together in pain until now.' This directly refers to the brute creation in what state this is at present we are now to consider.[42]

Similarly, a few years later, John Henry Newman, by then the most famous Roman Catholic in the country, remarked of Paley's *Natural Theology* in his 1852 lectures on *The Idea of a University*:

It has been taken out of its place, has been put too pro-minently forward, and thereby has almost been used as an instrument against Christianity . . . Physical [i.e. Natural] theology cannot . . . tell us one word about Christianity proper; it cannot be Christian, in any true sense, at all . . . [indeed] I do not hesitate to say that . . . this so-called science tends, if it occupies the mind, to dispose it against Christianity.[43]

Such objections to Paley did not occur to Darwin, however, as he immersed himself in the Archdeacon's cold, apparently incontrovertible reasoning. Paley's *Evidences* was a fitting counterpart to Sumner's *Evidence*. It piled on argument after argument: the sufferings of the first Christians, the authenticity of the Scriptures, the credibility of the miracles, the morality of the Gospels, the candour of the New Testament writers. 'The truth of Christianity depends upon [such] leading facts, and upon them alone . . . [and] of these we have evidence which ought to satisfy us,' Paley reasoned.[44] When combined with the detailed observation and seemingly irrefutable logic of *Natural Theology*, how could Darwin believe differently?

He could not. And yet it is clear that he still had doubts. It wasn't simply that he clearly preferred hunting and beetling to theology. It was more substantial. He could assent to William Paley's Christian reasoning, but how far was William Paley's Christian reasoning actually Christianity?

His friend, J. M. Herbert, who was also training for the ministry, recalled 'an earnest conversation' with Darwin 'about going into Holy Orders', in which Darwin expressed his doubts. During the ordination service the Bishop would ask candidates, 'Do you trust that you are inwardly moved by the Holy Spirit?' Herbert remembered Darwin asking him whether he could 'answer in the affirmative' when thus asked. Herbert replied that he could not, to which Darwin replied, 'Neither can I, and therefore I cannot take orders.'[45]

This reservation can be detected between the lines of a letter Darwin wrote to his cousin, William Fox, in April 1829. Fox's sister had died prematurely, and Darwin was writing with his condolences. 'I feel most sincerely & deeply for you & all your family,' he said. 'At the same time, as far as anyone can, by his own good principles & religion be supported under such a misfortune, you, I am assured, well know where to look for such support.' That was, of course, in the 'sympathy of all friends' but primarily in the 'pure & holy comfort the Bible affords'.[46]

It was, as his biographers Adrian Desmond and James Moore observe, a 'tortuous condolence', and although such letters are never easy to write, taken with Darwin's candid exchange with Herbert about not being 'inwardly moved by the Holy Spirit' it gets close to the heart of the kind of faith Darwin lost.

Darwin's pre-*Beagle* Christianity was a synthesis of Paley and Sumner: dogmatic, ordered, disciplined, reasonable, civilized, benign. It had limited time for revelation and virtually none for personal experience. Christ was not so much a person to be transformed by as a theorem to be proved. God was less the ground of our being, to which the sense of the sublime served as testimony, as he was the conclusion of a logical argument.

And the questions of suffering and injustice, keys in which the entire biblical symphony is written, had simply no place. Early nineteenth-century Anglican Christianity was a comfortable, confident 'happy world'. Small wonder Darwin scrabbled around so fruitlessly when faced with Fox's loss. If, as Janet Browne observes, 'the liberal, sceptical, easy-going blend of provincial Anglicanism and Unitarianism' that he took with him to Edinburgh could not offer him any spiritual or physical resolve when faced with the horrors of sickness and surgery, the confident, rational Paleyian Christianity he developed during his Cambridge years did little better.[47] His faith, such as it was, would offer him little defence against the suffering that would, in one way or another, feature prominently in his life and work.

Faith on the Beagle

Even while he was studying for the ministry, Darwin was planning for other eventualities. He had read Alexander von Humboldt's *Personal Journey* while at Cambridge and subsequently fantasized about exotic travel. He began to talk about setting up an expedition to Tenerife, which Humboldt had called a scientific paradise, in order to study its natural history. 'At present I talk, think and dream of a scheme I have almost hatched of going to the Canary Islands,' he told Fox in April 1831.[48]

In the end, something rather more substantial presented itself to him. In order to get his geology up to scratch for the Tenerife trip, his friend and teacher John Henslow asked Adam Sedgwick, Cambridge professor of geology, if he would take Darwin on one of his field trips. Sedgwick agreed and Darwin accompanied him for a week or so in August as he trekked through North Wales.

At about the same time, unknown to Darwin, one Captain Robert FitzRoy was seeking a suitable companion to accompany him on a trip that was likely to last years. FitzRoy, a lifelong naval man, was taking a ship, the *Beagle*, around South America on government business, charting coastal waters in order to improve their commercial potential for the nation. In this, he was simply completing the task begun by Captain Pringle Stokes several years earlier.

Stokes had taken the *Beagle* around the Tierra del Fuego in the 1820s. It was a grim experience. His maps were unreliable, his crew contracted scurvy, the weather was appalling, and the coastline desolate. Eventually, it all got too much for him. 'The soul of man dies in him,' he wrote in his logbook, before shooting himself.

FitzRoy stepped into the dead man's shoes, steering the *Beagle* round the remaining coastline and then returning home. That was to have been the end of the matter but friends and relatives at the Admiralty and the Hydrographer's Office decided that more work was needed and that FitzRoy was the man to do it.

FitzRoy was keen but wary. Captains did not socialize with their crews and the thought of years of cramped solitude surveying some of the bleakest coastlines on the planet had limited appeal. He was willing to share Captain Stokes' old cabin, but not his fate.

He petitioned the Hydrographer's Office to take an independent voyager with him, a gentleman with whom he would dine, share quarters and exchange erudite conversation. The authorities agreed, providing the voyager was financially independent, and feelers were put out. By a combination of chance and necessity, they settled on Darwin. Only certain scientifically minded gentlemen would do and Darwin was naturally among them, but he was not the first person approached and was nearly rejected by FitzRoy. FitzRoy was a keen phrenologist, believing that character could be ascertained by the shape and dimensions of an individual's head, and he didn't like the shape of Darwin's nose.

Once FitzRoy's fears had been assuaged, however, and Darwin's uncle Josiah had convinced his father that the journey would be a positive benefit for any future vicar, the deal was done. The *Beagle* sailed from Plymouth on 27 December 1831, taking Darwin on a journey that would last nearly five years and, in other ways, a lifetime.

Darwin was clear in his autobiography that while on board the *Beagle* he was 'quite orthodox'. He had planned to study the Greek New Testament on Sundays and, along with his shipmate Robert Hamond, specially requested Holy Communion from a chaplain in Buenos Aires before heading off for the dangerous Tierra del Fuego.

He also remembered 'being heartily laughed at by several of the officers . . . for quoting the Bible as an unanswerable authority on some point of morality'.[49] Having spent the last three years in Cambridge, Darwin naturally assumed that the Bible underpinned the social and moral order of the *Beagle* as it did the university.

To some extent he was right. The social stratification on board was rigid and pronounced. Captain FitzRoy was a religious man, although not as devout as he was later to become. Kindly to Darwin but brutally authoritarian towards his crew, and with a mercurial temper, he was variously liked, respected and feared. The crew were required to attend the weekly religious service he conducted. According to Darwin, they paid attention.

This was the kind of Christianity that Darwin was most comfortable with. Having attended a 'divine service' on board the *Warspite* when in Rio de Janeiro in July 1832, he remarked in his diary, 'the ceremony was imposing; especially the preliminary parts such as the "God save the King", when 650 men took off their hats'.[50] 'Seeing, when amongst foreigners, the strength & power of one's own Nation, gives a feeling of exultation which is not felt at home,' he added.

Not surprisingly, the few mentions of Christianity in Darwin's account and his diaries of the *Beagle* voyage relate primarily to its civilizing impact on indigenous people. To some extent this was a natural subject for him to comment on.

The *Beagle* was not simply a surveying ship, but was also a nascent mission, carrying on board the young Revd Richard Matthews, three Indians captured on the *Beagle*'s earlier voyage, and a great deal of equipment in order to set up a mission on the Tierra del Fuego. Missionary work would have been at the forefront of Darwin's mind.

The Christianity we read about in his diaries is a decent, English, civilizing force. Landing in Bahia in the north-east of Brazil in February 1832, Darwin found himself in a society where slavery was widespread. He had a deep and visceral loathing of slavery and came from resolutely abolitionist stock, both grandfathers having actively contributed to the anti-slavery campaigns of the 1780s and 90s. He was appalled by what he saw in Brazil, calling it, significantly, a 'scandal to Christian Nations'.[51] Slavery was not the kind of thing acceptable to Christian morality.

He was similarly appalled by the details of the Argentine war against the native Americans, recording in his diary for September 1833 that 'all the women who appear above twenty years old, are massacred in cold blood'. 'I ventured to hint,' he remarked, 'that this appeared rather inhuman.' His informant replied, 'Why what can be done, they breed so,' prompting Darwin to comment, 'Who would believe in this age in a Christian, civilized country that such atrocities were committed?'[52]

More happily, he had several encounters with missionaries in the South Pacific and their newly converted people and was, for the most part, mightily impressed. The *Beagle* landed in Tahiti in November 1835, remaining there for a week and a half. Darwin found the Tahitians as decent and civilized as the Fuegians (see 'Doubts on the *Beagle*: Fuegians' below) had been barbarous, a transformation due largely to the missionary work on the islands.

He was impressed by their piety. His *Voyage of the Beagle* tells of an excursion into the mountains while staying on the islands, led by several Tahitian guides. After a day's trekking and 'before we laid ourselves down to sleep':

the elder Tahitian fell on his knees, and with closed eyes repeated a long prayer in his native tongue. He prayed as a Christian should do, with fitting reverence, and without the fear of ridicule or any ostentation of piety.[53]

It was a similar story at mealtimes. 'At our meals neither of the men would taste food, without saying beforehand a short grace.' Such piety, Darwin remarked in an aside aimed at those critical of such missionary work, was genuine and heartfelt. 'Those travellers who think that a Tahitian prays only when the eyes of the missionary are fixed on him, should have slept with us that night on the mountain-side.'[54]

Nor was such piety simply 'religious'. Darwin recognized that the missionary work had had a very significant impact on Tahitian society. 'It appears to me that the morality and religion of the inhabitants is highly creditable,' he wrote. Those who attacked missionary work compared it with 'the high standard of Gospel perfection' and naturally found it wanting. Instead they should have been 'compar[ing] the present state with that of the island only twenty years ago'. 'They expect the missionaries to effect that which the Apostles themselves failed to do,' and naturally found them wanting.[55]

The reality was that 'human sacrifices . . . the power of an idolatrous priesthood . . . infanticide . . . [and] bloody wars, where the conquerors spared neither women nor children . . . have [all] been abolished' by missionary activity. Moreover, 'dishonesty, intemperance, and licentiousness have been greatly reduced by the introduction of Christianity'. Any voyager unlucky enough to be shipwrecked on some unknown coast should 'most devoutly pray' that missionaries had got there first.[56] 'The march of improvement, consequent on the introduction of Christianity through the South Sea, probably stands by itself on the records of the world.'[57]

It was a similar story in New Zealand, where the *Beagle* landed after Tahiti. 'I should think a more warlike race of inhabitants could not be found in any part of the world, than the New Zealanders,' Darwin commented in his account of the voyage. Yet 'at the present day, from the progress of civilization, there is much less warfare'. Again, this was due to the missionaries. Darwin recounted, for example, how a few years earlier:

A missionary found a chief and his tribe in preparation for war;— their muskets clean and bright, and their ammunition ready. He reasoned long on the inutility of the war, and the little provocation which had been given for it. The chief was much shaken in his resolution, and seemed in doubt.[58]

Alas, the missionary's efforts were to no avail as the chief then remembered that 'his gunpowder was in a bad state, and . . . would not keep much longer', so it might as well be used.

Unsuccessful as it might have been in this instance, missionary work had had a positive long-term impact. Darwin reckoned that the New Zealand missionary activity paid more attention to the 'direct improvement of the mind' of the indigenous people than did the Tahitian one, where 'more attention is there paid to religious instruction'. The impact was hardly less impressive for it, however.

As far as I was able to understand, the greater number of people in this northern part of the island profess Christianity. It is curious, that the religion even of those who do not profess it, has been modified and is now partly Christian, partly heathen. Moreover, so excellent is the Christian faith, that the outward conduct even of the unbelievers is said to have been decidedly improved by the spread of its doctrines.[59]

Ironically, it was the English residents, 'men of the most worthless character . . . addicted to drunkenness and all kinds of vice', who posed the greatest threat to the missionaries. Oddly enough, Darwin remarked, 'I have heard these worthy men say, that the only protection which they need . . . is from the native chiefs against Englishmen.'[60]

Darwin himself did his bit to defend the missionaries, in an article he co-authored with FitzRoy for the *South African Christian Recorder*, in the last months of his voyage. Stopping at the Cape of Good Hope in June 1836, Darwin found missionaries besieged by a rather different kind of attack. Critics were accusing them of failing to control the new converts, of exacerbating hostile racial conflicts between Dutch and British settlers and Bantu tribesmen, and of lining their own pockets by buying land cheap from natives and then selling it dear to Europeans.

> Much of the blame for the turmoil of the 1830s – the economic hardship following on from slave emancipation in 1833, the sixth frontier war of 1834, the Great Trek of 1835, the English legislation detailing the civil rights of the indigenous people – was unceremoniously laid at the doors of the African mission houses.[61]

Darwin and FitzRoy were reminded of similar criticisms of the mission stations that had so impressed them in Tahiti and New Zealand, and resolved to defend the South African missionaries in print. They wrote 'A letter, containing remarks on the moral state of Tahiti, New Zealand, &c', in which they defended missionary work in general and wrote glowingly of those missions they had recently seen.

> On the whole, balancing all that we have heard, and all that we ourselves have seen concerning the missionaries in the Pacific, we are very much satisfied that they thoroughly deserve the warmest support not only of individuals, but of the British Government.[62]

That the first article that Darwin published (at least intentionally – his friend Henslow had collated and published some of the scientific material from his letters in Darwin's absence) should have been a defence of missionary activity, and was written with a man whose subsequent view of the literality of

Genesis would put him at direct odds with the theory of evolution, is a matter of some irony.

Overall, Darwin's accounts of his *Beagle* years show how Christianity for him was not only a set of Paleyian propositions to which he intellectually assented, but was also a profoundly civilizing power, a force for morality and decency, one of Britain's finest exports.

Doubts on the Beagle: geology

It is easy to see the article in the *South African Christian Recorder* and Darwin's other comments on South Sea missionary activity as an indication that his Christian 'orthodoxy' remained strong right up until his return from the *Beagle*. That would be correct – although only partly so.

It would be unfair to characterize the *Beagle* years as simply ones of religious complacency. Just as the *Beagle* gave Darwin material for his theory of evolution but did not witness the formulation of that theory, so the voyage gave him the material for the loss of his Christian faith, without witnessing that loss. This happened in two areas in particular, the first being geology.

Darwin had gone on a geological crash course through the mountains of North Wales in the summer before he left on the *Beagle*. His companion, Adam Sedgwick, taught him much but was also critical of his fellow geological luminary, Charles Lyell, professor of geology at King's College, London. Sedgwick disliked Lyell's insistence that the earth's gradual, 'uniformitarian' changes were not directional. There was no obvious goal to the change, a fact that sat ill with the thoroughly directional conception of Christian history.

Darwin's friend Henslow was similarly sceptical, but recognized Lyell's importance and recommended to Darwin the first volume of Lyell's immensely influential *Principles of Geology* (the second and third volumes were yet to be published). He added some advice: Darwin was 'on no account to accept the views therein advocated'.[63]

FitzRoy made a present of the book to Darwin, who 'studied [it] attentively' and devoured the second and third volumes when he received them, in 1833 and 1834, with equal enthusiasm. Darwin ignored Henslow. He was impressed and deeply influenced.

'I am become a zealous disciple of Mr Lyell's views, as known in his admirable book,' he wrote to Fox towards the end of his voyage.[64] Recalling the books when writing to the geologist Leonard Horner nearly ten years later, he was even more effusive. 'I have always thought that the great merit of the *Principles*, was that it altered the whole tone of one's mind & therefore that when seeing a thing never seen by Lyell, one yet saw it partially through his eyes.'[65] Lyell's book, he wrote in his autobiography, 'was of the highest service to me in many ways . . . The science of Geology is enormously indebted to [him] – more so, as I believe, than to any other man who ever lived.'[66]

The influence on him was also theological. The new science of geology was being happily accommodated with religious belief even as early as the 1820s. The leading geologists of the day were mostly liberal Anglicans. On Darwin's account Lyell was 'thoroughly liberal in his religious beliefs or rather disbeliefs; but he was a strong theist'.[67] In good Paleyian fashion, Adam Sedgwick commented in his unpublished autobiographical notes, 'I am thankful that I have spent so much of my life in direct communion with nature, which is the reflection of the power, wisdom, and goodness of God,' a sentiment that was widely echoed by his peers.[68] Henslow himself was Professor of Mineralogy at Cambridge in the 1820s and also, in Darwin's own phrase, 'deeply religious, and so orthodox, that he told me one day, he should be grieved if a single word of the Thirty-nine Articles were altered'.[69]

The truth is that few of the leading British naturalists of the time believed in a literal, universal flood such as that described in Genesis chapter 7. Even the highly orthodox Henslow expressed doubts. Sedgwick's presidential address to the Geological Society in 1831 encouraged a metaphorical reading of the early chapters of Genesis, one that most leading naturalists and geologists were happy with. Even FitzRoy, later to become far more rigid and literalistic in his understanding of the Bible, was open to metaphorical readings at the time, reading Lyell and discussing geological theories with his learned shipmate. The shock that Darwin supposedly felt 'when during the *Beagle* voyage he first met someone who openly avowed disbelief in the flood', as recorded by his son George many years later, does not ring true.[70]

For all that, Darwin's immersion in Lyell and geology did unsettle his 'orthodox' belief. Lyell, while by no means antagonistic towards theology, did geology for geology's sake. He quietly 'ridiculed contemporary attempts to keep biblical truths to the fore when considering the history of the earth' and sought gently to reduce the natural theological thrust of the new science.[71] In the words of Janet Browne:

> To follow Lyell as slavishly as [Darwin] did in geological affairs was to become deeply impressed with the kind of secularized science offered by the Principles; and to adopt Lyell's wide-ranging philosophical programme was to free his mind to deal with personal belief in new ways.[72]

This, like Lyell's own theories, did not have a spectacular or catastrophic impact on Darwin's mind. Rather, it chipped away at its Paleyian foundations. Geology opened up to Darwin possibilities that lay beyond the world of William Paley.

His own experience did the same thing, only in a more direct way. In January 1835, while surveying Chiloe, a large island off the Chilean coast, the *Beagle* witnessed a volcanic eruption. Mount Osorno, 7,000 feet high, had been 'spouting out volumes of smoke' since Christmas, and at midnight on 19 January 'the sentry observed something like a large star; from which state the bright spot gradually increased in size till about three o'clock, when a very magnificent spectacle was presented'.[73] According to FitzRoy's account, 'Osorno was observed ... throwing up brilliant jets of flame or ignited matter, high into the darkness, while lava flowed down its steep sides in torrents, which from our distance (seventy-three miles) looked merely like red lines'.[74] Darwin may have been a thorough convert to Lyell's unspectacular 'uniformitarianism', the idea that geological change was slow and gradual rather than the result of periodic catastrophes, but this cannot have failed to make an impact on him. Osorno suggested that the earth was neither benign nor designed for man. Instead, it presented him with a ferocious and indifferent side to nature.

Much the same happened a month later when Darwin experienced a violent earthquake. The *Beagle* was in port at Valdivia, a small town on the Chilean coast. The crew were ashore, and Darwin 'lying down in [a] wood to rest myself' when the quake 'came on suddenly'. It lasted two minutes but its impact was enormous. Valdivia, built primarily of wood, survived largely intact but Concepción, a little further up the coast, was devastated. 'Not a house ... was standing,' a witness told him. 'Seventy villages were destroyed; and ... a great wave had almost washed away the ruins of Talcuhano'.[75] Darwin was soon able to observe the devastation for himself.

> The whole coast [was] strewed over with timber and furniture, as if a thousand great ships had been wrecked. Besides chairs, tables, bookshelves, &c., in great numbers, there were several roofs of cottages, which had been drifted in an almost entire state. The storehouses at Talcuhano had burst open, and great bags of cotton, yerba, and other valuable merchandise, were scattered about on the shore.[76]

Nature seemed wholly indifferent to human life. It was a disturbing event, provoking Darwin to write in his account of the voyage:

A bad earthquake at once destroys the oldest associations: the world, the very emblem of all that is solid, has moved beneath our feet like a crust over a fluid;—one second of time has conveyed to the mind a strange idea of insecurity, which hours of reflection would never have created.[77]

Such was the impact of geology on Darwin's faith. Lyell helped erode his Paleyian assumptions and natural disasters helped shake them. Neither was remotely capable of destroying his Christianity, but both cast shadows over the stable, ordered vision of nature that supposedly pointed directly to the deity that Darwin imbibed at Cambridge.

Doubts on the Beagle: Fuegians

The second challenge came from his experience of Fuegians. On his first journey around Tierra del Fuego, when he was completing Pringle Stokes' mission, FitzRoy had had a small boat, used for surveying the shallows, stolen by a band of Fuegians. In order to get it back he had taken a number of Fuegian hostages, most of whom managed to escape. Three remained, apparently unwilling to return, and FitzRoy hatched a plan.

He would bring them back to England, convert, educate and civilize them. He would then take them back so that they might set up an Anglican mission settlement in their homeland. FitzRoy purchased a fourth Fuegian, a boy aged about 14, for a single mother-of-pearl button (earning him the name Jemmy Button) but when one of the original hostages died of smallpox on return to England, the complement returned to three.

FitzRoy had been in the process of planning his return to Tierra del Fuego with his three Fuegians, Richard Matthews of the Church Mission Society and a wealth of generously donated but largely useless equipment to set up his mission, when he was commissioned to take the *Beagle* back to South America and complete its earlier work. His plans changed, but not too much. The three Fuegians and his plans for a mission settlement remained with him.

The Fuegians themselves were a mixed group. Yokcushlu, who came to be known as Fuegia Basket, was the youngest of the three, probably aged around 12 when they left Plymouth. 'A nice, modest, reserved young girl', according to Darwin, she had a 'rather pleasing but sometimes sullen expression, and [was] very quick in learning anything, especially languages'.[78]

Orundellico, latterly known as James or Jemmy Button, was a little older. He was 'a universal favourite' of the crew. 'Short, thick, and fat', according to Darwin, he was also rather 'vain of his personal appearance'. He liked wearing gloves, had his hair neatly cut, and 'was distressed if his well-polished shoes were dirtied'. He was 'merry and often laughed', 'remarkably sympathetic with any one in pain', and inordinately 'fond of admiring himself in a looking-glass'.[79]

The third Fuegian was called El'leparu but became known as York Minster. He was older than the other two, probably born around 1804, and less popular. Darwin described him as 'a full-grown, short, thick, powerful man'. 'His disposition was reserved, taciturn, morose, and when excited violently passionate'.[80]

FitzRoy had had his three charges studied intensively when in England and noted, in his 'Phrenological Remarks on Three Fuegians', appended to his account of the voyage, that each had a reasonably strong sense of the divine. Yokcushlu had 'strong feelings for a Supreme Being' and Orundellico 'will manifest strong feelings for a Supreme Being'. El'leparu, by comparison, 'will not have such strong feelings for the Deity as his two companions'.[81]

Darwin had no interest in phrenology and failed to detect any such strong religious sentiments from his more conventional observations. Nor, moreover, did he think FitzRoy had been able to. Silent on the subject in the first edition of the *Voyage*, Darwin remarked in the second that:

> Captain FitzRoy could never ascertain that the Fuegians have any distinct belief in a future life. They sometimes bury their dead in caves, and sometimes in the mountain forests; [but] we do not know what ceremonies they perform.[82]

Jemmy Button 'would not eat land-birds, because "eat dead men" ', and none of the three were willing 'even to mention their dead friends'. 'We have no reason to believe that they perform any sort of religious worship', Darwin continued, 'though perhaps the muttering of the old man before he distributed the putrid blubber to his famished party, may be of this nature,' he added colourfully.[83]

The 'nearest approach to a religious feeling' that he encountered was shown by York Minster, who, when one of the crew shot some very young ducklings as specimens, declared in the most solemn manner, 'Oh Mr. Bynoe, much rain, snow, blow much.' This, Darwin concluded, 'was evidently a retributive punishment for wasting human food'.[84]

This apparent absence of religious motivation (although it would be hard to claim that Darwin's casual observations were much more reliable than FitzRoy's phrenology) clearly made an impression on the naturalist. Thirty years later he wrote in *The Descent of Man*:

> There is no evidence that man was aboriginally endowed with the ennobling belief in the existence of an Omnipotent God. On the contrary there is ample evidence, derived not from hasty travellers, but from men who have long resided with savages, that numerous races have existed and still exist, who have no idea of one or more gods, and who have no words in their languages to express such an idea.[85]

This was more than just a detached observation, as a remark he made in his autobiography shows:

At the present day the most usual argument for the existence of an intelligent God is drawn from the deep inward conviction and feelings which are experienced by most persons. But ... there are ... many barbarian tribes who cannot be said with any truth to believe in what we call God.[86]

So much store had been placed, in works of natural theology, on the way in which a universal religious sentiment pointed clearly in the direction of the Judeo-Christian God, that it was no surprise that Darwin's experience of the Fuegians' very different or perhaps non-existent religious sentiments should cast questions over his own beliefs.

Similar questions were posed by his first encounter with native Fuegians in January 1833. It was shocking. 'I shall never forget how wild and savage one group appeared,' he remarked.

Four or five men came to the edge of an overhanging cliff; they were absolutely naked, and their long hair streamed about their faces; they held rugged staffs in their hands, and, springing from the ground, they waved their arms round their heads, and sent forth the most hideous yells.[87]

'A wild man is indeed a miserable animal,' he remarked to Fox a few months later.[88]

The mission was established, and Matthews left with Fuegia Basket, York Minster, Jemmy Button and their 'provisions': 'wine glasses, butter-bolts, tea-trays, soup turins, [a] mahogany dressing case, fine white linen, beavor hats & an endless variety of similar things'. It was, Darwin remarked, a 'choice of articles [that] showed the most culpable folly & negligence'.[89]

Perhaps not surprisingly the mission was a disaster. When the *Beagle* returned to the settlement a month later, Matthews was in state of nervous collapse. According to Darwin's diary, 'from the moment of our leaving, a regular system of plunder commenced'. Matthews had lost nearly everything. Worse, he was continually hassled by Fuegians who surrounded his house 'night & day'.[90]

Thinking they were after more of his provisions, Matthews 'met them with presents'. But it wasn't enough. The Fuegians indicated that they wanted to 'strip him & pluck all the hairs out of his face & body'. 'I think we returned just in time to save his life,' Darwin observed.[91]

Matthews scrambled on board but none of the captive Fuegians wanted to return to the Beagle. FitzRoy was downhearted and Matthews distraught. Darwin's own feelings are not recorded but it is clear that the entire Fuegian saga made a lasting impact on him. Browne remarks that of all his experiences during the voyage, 'it was this recognition of the connections between humans around the world that moved him the most . . . He was forced to acknowledge that the gauzy film of culture was nothing but an outer garment for humanity, acquired or lost in response to the individual milieu.'[92] It gave him a feeling of 'theological relativity'.[93] If the eruption and earthquake along the Chilean coast suggested to him that the world was not necessarily what he assumed it to be, his experiences round Tierra del Fuego said the same thing of human beings.

Conclusion

In the decade and a half following his return from the Beagle, Darwin lost his Christian faith. But that faith had been of a particular type, a type that smoothed the path for its subsequent loss.

On 5 September 1834, Darwin was travelling through Chile, a few miles south of Santiago. In the evening he and his companions reached a comfortable farmhouse 'where there were several very pretty señoritas'.[94] Throughout his travels Darwin had often stopped off to 'admire the brilliancy of the decorations' of the gloriously baroque Catholic churches of the continent. 'It is impossible not to respect the fervour which appears to reign during the Catholic service as compared with the Protestant,' he remarked in his diary.[95]

He mentioned his aesthetically motivated churchgoing to his pretty señoritas and was taken aback by their shock.

> They were much horrified at my having entered one of their churches out of mere curiosity [and] asked me, 'Why do you not become a Christian—for our religion is certain?' I assured them I was a sort of Christian.[96]

Darwin meant, of course, an Anglican *sort* of Christian rather than a Roman Catholic one. But the phrase 'a sort of Christian' has connotations beyond its intended usage. In many ways it serves as an apt if accidental description of the whole Christian faith he lost.

That Christian faith was genuine. Any attempt to show that Darwin wasn't *really* a Christian before or during his *Beagle* days would be an exercise in sophistry. Darwin was a confirmed Christian and an Anglican one at that. He immersed himself in the writings of Anglican theologians and assented to the creeds and the Thirty-nine Articles, although he later wrote that 'It never struck me how illogical it was to say that I believed in what I could not understand and what is in fact unintelligible.'[97]

That recognized, Darwin was a particular *sort* of Christian, a sort typical of his time and class.

His was a Christian faith that was founded squarely on the arguments of Sumner and Paley: objective, rationalistic, demonstrable. It was a Christian faith that drew its energy and confidence from the world about it, preferring the supposedly incontestable evidence of natural theology over the contentious and controversial ones of scripture and theology. It was a faith that eschewed religious experience, as both intellectually unreliable and personally unappealing. And it was a faith that was very much of its culture: civilized, ordered, comfortable, decent.

None of this is to criticize that faith. It would have been unusual for a man of his upbringing, class and personal concerns to have believed in any other sort of way. Rather, it is to understand the Christianity he had up until the age of 27, when he returned from the *Beagle* and entered upon the most intense period of brilliant and radical speculation of his whole life. And it is to understand why that period and what followed it had the effect on his faith that it did.

2

'The concealed war': losing his religion

The *Beagle* returned to England on 2 October 1836, and Darwin headed straight for Shrewsbury. Ten days later he left for Cambridge and thereafter London, where he met with many of the scientifically minded men with whom he had corresponded over the previous five years.

The next two years were spent shuttling between London and Cambridge, analysing the specimens he had brought back with him, filling notebooks with speculation and preparing his account of the voyage. It was a busy time, but one in which he found time to think about marriage.

Before the *Beagle*, Darwin had been romantically inclined towards Fanny Owen, the daughter of an old family friend, but she had married not long after he had departed, leaving him (briefly) broken-hearted. He was now back and hearing the call of marriage and domesticity.

Marriage was not inevitable, of course – his elder brother Erasmus was never to wed – and nor was it necessarily desirable. There were pros and cons to be considered. In typical fashion, Darwin considered them, scribbling 'This is the Question' across the top of a scrap of paper, tentatively dated to July 1838, and then drawing up two columns, one headed 'Marry' and the other 'Not Marry':

Marry	Not Marry
Children – (if it Please God) – Constant companion, (& friend in old age) who will feel interested in one, – object to be beloved & played with. – better than a dog anyhow. – Home, & someone to take care of house – Charms of music & female chit-chat. – These things good for one's health. – ~~Forced to visit &~~ ~~receive relations~~ *but terrible loss of time.* – ~~W~~ My God, it is intolerable to think of spending ones whole life, like a neuter bee, working, working, & nothing after all. – No, no won't do. – Imagine living all one's day solitarily in smoky dirty London House. – Only picture to yourself a nice soft wife on a sofa with good fire, & books & music perhaps – Compare this vision with the dingy reality of Grt. Marlbro' St.	No children, (no second life), no one to care for one in old age. – What is the use of working '~~in~~' without sympathy from near & dear friends – who are near & dear friends to the old, except relatives

Freedom to go where one liked – choice of Society & *little of it.* – Conversation of clever men at clubs – Not forced to visit relatives, & to bend in every trifle. – to have the expense & anxiety of children – perhaps quarelling – Loss of time. – cannot read in the Evenings – fatness & idleness – Anxiety & responsibility – less money for books &c – if many children forced to gain one's bread. – (But then it is very bad for ones health to work too much)

Perhaps my wife wont like London; then the sentence is banishment & degradation into indolent, idle fool – |

There were arguments on both sides but it was clear which option won. 'Marry – Marry – Marry Q.E.D.' he wrote at the bottom of the page.

Marriage and doubts

The question was whom. Darwin had long been close to his cousins, the Wedgwoods, and was a frequent visitor to their house at Maer. Towards the end of 1837 he began to take an interest in Emma. She was a year older than him, knew French, Italian and German, played the piano and had fended off numerous marriage proposals while he was at sea. She was also devout, her Christian faith being both sincere and extremely important to her.

Her family's Unitarian background, with its emphasis on inner feeling over scripture or dogma, provided the foundation for her personal beliefs which, while simple, were not simplistic, being the product of serious reading and questioning. Most influential, however, was the death of her sister Fanny in August 1832, aged only 26. Emma was deeply upset and lived in hope of meeting her once again. 'Oh, Lord, help me to become more like her, and grant that I may join her with Thee never to part again,' she wrote shortly after the death.[98]

Darwin courted Emma and spoke to his father. Religion had been a point of tension between the Wedgwoods and Darwins ever since grandfather Erasmus had gently mocked Josiah Wedgwood's Unitarianism. Moreover, Darwin's father knew something of his son's growing scepticism, a scepticism that he undoubtedly shared. He counselled caution. 'Before I was engaged to be married, my father advised me to conceal carefully my doubts, for he said that he had known extreme misery thus caused with married persons,' Darwin recalled in his autobiography.[99]

Darwin was nothing if not an honest man, however, and on a visit to Maer in July 1838 he confided in Emma. 'He is the most open, transparent man I ever saw, and every word expresses his real thoughts,' she later wrote to her aunt.[100] There is no record of what Darwin told her or what her immediate reaction was, but it clearly caused some difficulties, and occasioned a series of letters and notes from Emma to Charles that, happily for biographers, give a good and contemporary glimpse of his fading Christian faith at the time. The difficulties were clearly not too serious, however, as six months later the couple were married.

In her first letter on the matter, dated November 1838, Emma wrote that although when together 'all melancholy thoughts keep out of my head', when apart 'some sad ones . . . force themselves in'. She thanked him 'from my heart' for his openness, and said how she should dread the idea that he was 'concealing . . . opinions from the fear of giving me pain'. Nevertheless, she was open about her fear that 'our opinions on the most important subject should differ widely'. 'My reason', she wrote, 'tells me that honest & conscientious doubts cannot be a sin,' and she certainly believed him to be honest and conscientious. Nevertheless, she knew enough about his mind and interests to worry about the direction his doubts were taking him. So she asked him for a favour. 'Read our Saviour's farewell discourse to his disciples which begins at the end of the 13th Chap of John,' she asked. 'It is so full of love to them & devotion & every beautiful feeling. It is the part of the New Testament I love best.' In her own gentle and tentative way, she was asking him to open himself up to evidence and, more importantly, experience that she sensed was somehow off limits.[101]

Two months later she mentioned the matter again, briefly, saying that while 'our opinions may not agree upon all points of religion', she hoped that 'we may sympathize a good deal in our feelings on the subject'.[102] A little while later, shortly after they were married on 29 January 1839, she wrote him her fullest note on the subject. Unable to 'say exactly what I wish to say', she put her thoughts on paper.

She began by confirming her earlier sentiments, saying she felt that 'while you are acting conscientiously & sincerely wishing & trying to learn the truth, you cannot be wrong'. However, she confided, 'there are some reasons that force themselves upon me & prevent my being always able to give myself this comfort'.[103]

In essence, Emma believed that Darwin was not giving the evidence for Christianity a fair hearing. First, he simply didn't give it sufficient time.

Your mind & time are full of the most interesting subjects & thoughts of the most absorbing kind, viz following up yr own discoveries – but which make it very difficult for you to avoid casting out as interruptions other sorts of thoughts which have no relation to what you are pursuing or to make it possible for [you] to be able to give your whole attention to both sides of the question.

He was becoming so obsessed with his subject that he was devaluing or simply ignoring that which might offer other perspectives on life.

Second, he was prejudiced as to what constituted legitimate evidence.

It seems to me also that the line of your pursuits may have led you to view chiefly the difficulties on one side, & that you have not had time to consider & study the chain of difficulties on the other . . . I should say . . . that there is a danger in giving up revelation.

Third, consciously or not, he was demanding proof for a subject that did not lend itself to proof. Evidence was one thing; proof quite another.

May not the habit in scientific pursuits of believing nothing till it is proved, influence your mind too much in other things which cannot be proved in the same way, & which if true are likely to be above our comprehension.

This was no harangue. 'I do not wish for any answer to all this,' she concluded. 'It is a satisfaction to me to write it.' Moreover, it was deeply felt and emotionally expressed.

Every thing that concerns you concerns me & I should be most unhappy if I thought we did not belong to each other forever ... I cannot tell [you] how happy [you] make me & how dearly I love [you] & thank [you] for all [your] affection which makes the happiness of my life more & more every day.

It was clearly received in a similar spirit. Some time later, Darwin scrawled in ink beneath the note, 'When I am dead, know that many times, I have kissed & cryed over this.' But it did not have any lasting impact.

'I gradually came to disbelieve ...'

The years 1837–9 were crucial in Darwin's loss of faith, and Emma's letters offer an invaluable perspective on the period. Darwin's own account, such as it is, is located in a short chapter entitled 'Religious Belief' in his autobiography. This is positioned after a chapter entitled 'From my return to England Oct. 2, 1836 to my marriage Jan. 29, 1839', and begins, 'during these two years I was led to think much about religion', so it is clear that it refers, at least in theory, to the same period. It is very different from Emma's letters, however, and worth comparing with them.[104]

Darwin begins by saying how orthodox he was on the *Beagle*, before listing, albeit briefly, the ways in which he came to doubt the Christian faith in this period. These fell into three categories.

First, there were scriptural doubts. Although he offers no details of how he came to change his mind, he wrote that 'by this time, [I had come] to [doubt] the Old Testament [with] its manifestly false history of the world, with the Tower of Babel, the rainbow as a sign, etc.'. The problem was similar, if less acute, for the New Testament, as 'the Gospels cannot be proved to have been written simultaneously with the events ... [and] they differ in many important details, far too important ... to be admitted as the usual inaccuracies of eye-witnesses'. Darwin claimed that he was 'very unwilling to give up my belief' and recalled 'often inventing day-dreams of old letters between distinguished Romans and manuscripts being discovered at Pompeii or elsewhere which confirmed in the most striking manner all that was written in the Gospels'. It was to no avail.

Second, there were moral objections. Darwin saw the Old Testament writers 'attribute to God the feelings of a revengeful tyrant', and concluded that it 'was no more to be trusted than the sacred books of the Hindoos, or the beliefs of any barbarian'. The New Testament, 'beautiful as is [its] morality', was insufficient compensation, not least because he felt too much 'depends . . . on the interpretation which we now put on metaphors and allegories'. More broadly, he expressed a profound objection to the doctrine of eternal hellfire. 'The plain language of the text seems to show that the men who do not believe, and this would include my Father, Brother and almost all my best friends, will be everlastingly punished. And this is a damnable doctrine.'

Finally, there were philosophical problems. Following in the steps of eighteenth-century philosophers, Darwin argued that the same miracles that had so impressed William Paley were simply incredible. 'The clearest evidence would be requisite to make any sane man believe in the miracles by which Christianity is supported.' 'The more we know of the fixed laws of nature the more incredible do miracles become.' 'Men at that time were ignorant and credulous to a degree almost incomprehensible by us.' The reasons mounted up.

'By such reflections as these,' he summarized, 'I gradually came to disbelieve in Christianity as a divine revelation.'

It is not always clear how we should read Darwin's autobiography. It was written for his immediate family rather than for public consumption and was sensitive enough not to be published in full until 1958, Emma having requested certain passages be excised from the initial publication. At the same time, there is clearly a degree of manipulation within it, to the extent that his biographer Janet Browne has written that it 'was just as much an exercise in camouflage – a disguise – as it was a methodical laying out of the bare bones of his existence'.[105]

It is difficult to say how much this was the case in this particular matter. Darwin's scepticism towards biblical historicity, for example, seems entirely credible. Doubting the veracity of the Bible was almost a pastime of Victorian intellectuals. One should not, however, overstate the level of Darwin's biblical knowledge. It was not until 1861 that he realized that the marginal notation in standard editions of the English Bible that claimed that the world began in 4004 BC was not actually in the Bible but derived from the seventeenth-century biblical chronology of James Ussher, Archbishop of Armagh.[106] Moreover, the fact that the two examples he cites in his autobiography are the Tower of Babel and the flood also raises suspicions. The literality of the opening chapters of Genesis had already been profoundly questioned by the (ordained) geologists who so influenced him in the 1830s. It seems unlikely that Darwin believed them completely and without question prior to 1837–9.

Similar problems abound with his comments on the New Testament. Again, although his scepticism relating to the Gospels' accuracy is credible, it is unlikely he felt it as early as 1837–9. New Testament scholarship can be traced back into the eighteenth century, but it only really began in earnest in Germany in the 1820s and only began to make an impact in Britain from the 1840s. The re-evaluation of Jesus that led poets like Arthur Hugh Clough to write desperately, 'He is not risen, no,/He lies and moulders low;/Christ is not risen', had hardly touched British society by the 1830s.[107] That particular melancholy, long, withdrawing roar of faith was still a decade or more away. Thus, while there is no reason to doubt that Darwin was sceptical of the Gospels' authenticity and reliability, it seems unlikely that he developed that scepticism between 1837 and 1839, and certainly not as comprehensively as he suggests. It is more probable that he telescoped his subsequent scepticism into a period of intense and destabilizing intellectual activity.

Fewer queries surround his moral doubts about the God of the Old Testament. Such opinions were common in the period, Charles Dickens, for example, loathing the Old Testament but loving the New. Much the same could be said about his attitude to the doctrine of hell, which itself underwent a significant re-evaluation in the Victorian period. Similarly, his opinion of miracles came straight from the pages of the influential Scottish sceptic David Hume, and resonates entirely with his own notebook speculations on the law-governed nature of life.

The likelihood is, therefore, that Darwin fashioned his autobiography at this point in order to bring together all his doubts into a single chapter and timeframe. His own comment that 'disbelief crept over me at a very slow rate' suggests as much, and indicates that there was a degree of selection and creativity at work. That recognized, there is little reason to doubt that when, in the 1870s, he looked back at his life and tried to explain his loss of Christian faith, these factors loomed large. That they were overshadowed by one other factor, which is all but passed over in the autobiography, is an issue to which we shall return.

What is particularly interesting in Darwin's account of his loss of faith is the factual, almost propositional nature of the faith he lost. According to his own reading, whereas he had once been able to put ticks alongside Old Testament historicity, Gospel veracity, miracles and so on, in precisely the way that studying William Paley or John Sumner would have encouraged him to, he could no longer do so. These were propositions to which he could no longer grant assent. By his own account, the Christian faith he lost was a series of arguments, rather than an experience of God.

In this way, Emma's comments about her husband's threadbare faith over 1838–9 do not so much contradict his own reckoning as complement it. For Darwin, Christianity had been primarily, if not quite exclusively, a set of ideas to which he gave intellectual assent. His account of his loss of religious beliefs naturally, therefore, took that angle. Emma's own account is different, reflecting her understanding of Christianity and offering a telling perspective on the way his mind worked.

For Emma the issue was not so much what he believed in (she said surprisingly little about this) but his attitude to belief in the first place. His mind was fast becoming what he was later to call 'a kind of machine for grinding general laws out of large collections of facts', and she recognized that this was lethal to religious faith.[108] It was not that she advocated belief *in spite* of the evidence – she repeatedly emphasized how she was open to the validity of conscientious and honest enquiry – but rather that she called for a broader and more generous concept of what constituted evidence. Put bluntly, she recognized that if he automatically disqualified personal feeling or experience as legitimate evidence, or automatically disallowed the concept of revelation, or demanded of texts the same kind of proof that he did of biological specimens, it was almost inevitable that he should lose whatever Christian faith he had.

To a degree, Darwin himself recognized this in his autobiography. After recollecting his daydreams about finding unimpeachable historical confirmation of the Gospels, he remarked that, 'I found it more and more difficult, with free scope given to my imagination, to invent evidence which would suffice to convince me.' Nothing was likely to satisfy his evidential demands. He wanted proof, but to a mind that had become attuned to interrogating specimen after specimen after specimen, no historical evidence could conceivably provide proof. The New Testament texts were thus set a task they could not, by definition, fulfil.

For all their different perspectives, Emma's and her husband's accounts do accord in one important detail. The Victorian era is famous for pained (and affected) crises of faith. It is ironic that Darwin, who indirectly prompted so many of these, felt no such crisis himself. He wrote in his autobiography that he did not think that 'the religious sentiment was ever strongly developed in me'. As a result, when 'disbelief crept over' him at such a slow rate he felt 'no distress'.

Emma's note to him following their marriage supports this account. Recounting one of their conversations, she wrote:

> I do not quite agree with you in what you once said — that luckily there were no doubts as to how one ought to act. I think prayer is an instance to the contrary, in one case it is a positive duty & perhaps not in the other. But I dare say you meant in actions which concern others & then I agree with you almost if not quite.[109]

Her comments are revealing. Darwin had clearly expressed to her the opinion that whether one believed in the Christian creeds or not made precious little difference to how one ought to behave – a comment that could only have been made by a man so deeply embedded in an all-encompassing, Christian culture that he could not conceive of other moral outlooks. It was obvious how one ought to behave. What sane man could doubt it? The sentiments expose the English, civilizing Christianity that Darwin had exhibited and applauded on board the *Beagle*. So obvious and plentiful were the fruits of moral decency and propriety that Darwin dismissed the idea they grew on a particular creedal tree. Were he to have seen the ways his own theory of evolution would be used and abused to justify market fundamentalism, racism and ultimately genocide, he might have been less sanguine.

More broadly, his comments also show that his loss of faith was not that much of a loss. Yes, he could no longer assent to various Christian claims. Yes, he doubted the immortality of the soul. But he did not, as yet, question the existence of God, still less the rightness of Christian morality. His loss of faith need not make a material difference to how he lived his life.

Notes and queries

The scriptural, moral and philosophical doubts that Darwin locates in the period 1837–9 are likely to have taken place over a longer and less clearly defined timeframe. What undoubtedly did occur over those years was a period of intense and radical speculation that Darwin captured, in fragmented form, in a series of notebooks.

These were begun in 1837 and encompassed speculations on geology, evolution, metaphysics, morals and human expression. These notebooks, more than anything else, reveal Darwin's thoughts and trace the origin and development of his theory. They only rarely deal directly with religious questions, still less his personal religious beliefs, but they are essential to any understanding of Darwin's mind over this formative period.[110]

At the same time, Darwin began reading widely, noting in his journal for August 1838 that he 'paid some attention to Metaphysical subjects' and for the following month that he 'read a good deal on many subjects [and] thought much upon religion'. The books included works by Adam Smith, John Locke, Sir Thomas Browne, David Hume, and (at least a review of) Auguste Comte's *Positive Philosophy*. Hume clearly shaped his opinion of miracles, as intimated in his autobiography, and Comte influenced his understanding of human development. Comte argued that society passes through three stages – the theological, metaphysical and scientific – which corresponded broadly with the known history of Europe. His ideas, although later savaged by Darwin's friend Thomas Huxley, connected with Darwin's own emphasis on mutability and development and made him 'think deeply'. He referred to them in his notebooks as a way of understanding the mentality of the 'savages ([like] York Minster)', and they clearly made a deep impression on him, as he was quoting them years later when engaged in an ongoing debate on the role, if any, of God in evolution. 'I must think that such views of Asa Gray & Herschel merely show that the subject in their minds is in Comte's theological stage of science,' he wrote to Charles Lyell many years later.[111]

Neither Darwin's notebooks nor his reading was systematic, and they do not offer us a complete or concise picture of his mind at the time. What they do reveal, in fragments, is an intellect that was vigorously questioning the foundations of pretty much every orthodoxy of the time. It is these speculations that underlie the otherwise inexplicable transition, evident in his autobiography, from the orthodox Christian of the *Beagle* to the full-fledged sceptic of two years later.

In the first instance, the more he read and thought, the less credence Darwin could give to special creation, the idea that the species were created (by God) in their current form. Not only did such an idea sit uneasily alongside what he had observed and collected on the *Beagle*, but it explained nothing. 'The explanation of types of structure in classes – as resulting from the will of the deity, to create animals on certain plans, – is no explanation,' he noted in response to John Macculloch's book, *Proofs and Illustrations of the Attributes of God*. 'It has not the character of a physical law & is therefore utterly useless. – it foretells nothing because we know nothing of the will of the Deity.'

Macculloch had argued, after William Paley, that species had been created to fit certain environmental niches. Thus he had a 'long rigmarole about plants being created to arrest mud etc at deltas'. But Darwin's theory of natural selection dispensed with this argument. Paley's foundations were being fatally undermined.

Darwin's faith may have been likewise weakened, but it was far from destroyed. The same commentary on Macculloch's argument sees Darwin expressing a view that others were to make after him. 'If we were to presume that God created plant[s] to arrest earth, (like a Dutchman plants them to stop the moving sand) we lower the creator to the standard of one of his weak creations.'

This was important. No longer believing in special creation did not destroy Darwin's religious faith. Indeed, he clearly thought that special creation was a clumsier and uglier idea than the alternative. 'Has the Creator since the Cambrian formation gone on creating animals with [the] same general structure,' he asked rhetorically in Notebook B. What a 'miserable limited view', he exclaimed.

How much more magnificent a view, he wrote in Notebook D, was a vision of 'Astronomical causes, modified by unknown ones [which] cause changes in geography & changes of climate ... then superadded [to] changes of form in the organic world'. Such changes 'affect each other, & their bodies by certain laws of harmony keep perfect in these themselves – instincts alter, reason is formed & the world peopled with myriads of distinct forms from a period short of eternity to the present time, to the future'.

How much 'grander' was this 'than [the] idea from cramped imagination that God created ... the Rhinoceros of Java & Sumatra [and] that since the time of the Silurian he has made a long succession of vile molluscous animals'? Such a vision of God was hardly very divine. 'How beneath the dignity of him, who is supposed to have said let there be light & there was light.'

In his own, fragmentary notes, Darwin was articulating the same view that Charles Kingsley would one day express more eloquently in a letter praising *The Origin of Species*, parts of which Darwin would subsequently include in the second edition of that book.

> I have gradually learnt to see that it is just as noble a conception of Deity, to believe that he created primal forms capable of self development ... as to believe that He required a fresh act of intervention to supply the lacunas [or 'gaps'] which he himself had made.[112]

Reconciling his new, evolutionary view of life with Christianity demanded more than this, however. Philosophically and aesthetically more satisfying as his theory of transmutation, as it was then called, may have been, Darwin recognized there were other issues. 'Once grant that species . . . may pass into each other . . . & the whole fabric totters & falls,' he noted in Notebook C. Evolution had serious implications for humans.

In March 1838, Darwin went to the Zoological Society in London, where he saw 'the Ourang-outang in great perfection'. It was a fascinating encounter.

> The keeper showed her an apple, but would not give it her, whereupon she threw herself on her back, kicked & cried, precisely like a naughty child. – She then looked very sulky & after two or three fits of passion, the keeper said, 'Jenny if you will stop bawling & be a good girl, I will give you the apple.' – She certainly understood every word of this, &, though like a child, she had great work to stop whining, she at last succeeded, & then got the apple, with which she jumped into an arm chair & began eating it, with the most contented countenance imaginable.[113]

Darwin's account, given in a letter to his sister Susan, underlines (as if it were needed) how close he felt humans and other primates were. The encounter occasioned further speculations in Notebook B.

> Let man visit Ourang-outang in domestication, hear expressive whine, see its intelligence when spoken [to]; as if it understands every word said – see its affection – to those it knew – see its passion & rage, sulkiness & very actions of despair; let him look at savage, roasting his parent, naked, artless, not improving yet improvable & let him dare to boast of his proud pre-eminence.

What was being challenged here was not so much man's uniqueness as his dignity. Time and again in his notebooks, Darwin attacks the idea that there is some kind of infinite qualitative difference between mankind and other animals. In spite of superficial appearances, humans were also creatures.

'It is absurd to talk of one animal being higher than another,' he noted in Notebook B. '*We* consider . . . the intellectual faculties . . . as highest.' But such a view was arrogant and anthropocentric. 'A bee doubtless would [consider differently].' 'When we talk of higher orders, we should always say intellectually higher. — But who with the face of the earth covered with the most beautiful savannahs and forests dare to say that intellectuality is [the] only aim in this world.'

'Man – wonderful man . . . with divine face turned towards heaven . . . he is not a deity, his end under present form will come . . . he is no exception,' he wrote in Notebook C, sounding almost like an Old Testament prophet. 'He possesses some of the same general instincts & feelings as animals.'

Such speculations bruised human pride, but there was more. Evolution had implications beyond merely denting mankind's sense of superiority. 'He who understands [a] baboon would do more toward metaphysics than Locke,' Darwin suggested in Notebook M. Plato's *Phaedo* claims that 'our "imaginary ideas" arise from the pre-existence of the soul, [and] are not derivable from experience', he wrote elsewhere, before adding decisively: 'read monkeys for pre-existence'.

If man was an animal among animals, that which appeared instinctive among them was also, presumably, instinctive among us – including, it would seem, thought itself. 'Why is thought being a secretion of brain, more wonderful than gravity a property of matter?' he asked in Notebook C. Only 'our arrogance . . . our admiration of ourselves' caused us to think otherwise.

'Thought, however unintelligible it may be, seems as much [a] function of organ, as bile of liver,' he speculated in Notebook N. 'Is the attraction of carbon, hydrogen in certain definite proportions (different from what takes place out of bodies) really less wonderful than thoughts,' he went on. And in any case, 'What is matter?' he asked, stopping at a question he would later reject as simply unanswerable.

Ultimately Darwin recognized that if 'the mind is [a] function of body', and thinking were merely an 'instinct . . . [that] result[s] from [the] organization of [the] brain', how could we know we can trust our thoughts? The notebooks do not offer much of an answer, and the question would re-emerge in Darwin's informal metaphysical musings in the last decades of his life.

If thinking could be reduced to the 'merely' material, so could morality. Perhaps morality was merely an instinct too? Worse, perhaps it was an imperfectly formed and harmful instinct. 'The mind of man is no more perfect than instincts of animals to all & changing contingencies, or bodies of either,' Darwin thought. 'Our descent, then, is the origin of our evil passions!! —The Devil under form of Baboon is our grandfather!' If all this were true, it seemed to suggest that good and evil were not moral absolutes rooted in a spiritual realm, but primate attributes on which humans have stumbled.

As if this weren't bad enough, hovering just behind such speculations was the aged spectre of free will or, rather, the lack of it. 'My wish to improve my temper, what does it arise from, but organization,' he asked. 'That organization may have been affected by circumstances & education & by the choice which at that time organization gave me to will.' 'Verily the faults of the fathers, corporeal & bodily, are visited upon the children.'

It need hardly be said that doubting free will had enormous implications for religious faith. 'A man hearing bible by chance becomes good,' he reasoned. But if 'this is effect of accident with his state of desire (neither by themselves sufficient) effect of birth & other accidents: [he] may be congratulated, but deserves no credit'. What, then, would happen to the whole balance sheet of good and evil that underpinned the entire Christian moral universe, as Darwin understood it?

To this he added concerns relating to the supposed ubiquity of religious sensibility. His experiences around the Tierra del Fuego raised their head. Referring to his brother-in-law, he remarked in Notebook C, 'Hensleigh says the love of the deity & thought of him or eternity only difference between the mind of man & animals.' 'Yet how faint in a Fuegian or Australian!' he exclaimed.

This particular difficulty was not insurmountable. 'Why not gradation,' he asked. Surely it was 'no greater difficulty for [the] Deity to choose when [primates became] perfect enough for future state', than to choose 'when good enough for Heaven or bad enough for Hell'. Indeed, he added in parenthesis, he may even have witnessed the evolution of such religious sensibility on his journey, citing how the stories that York Minster and others told showed 'glimpses bursting on mind & giving rise to the wildest imagination & superstition'.

Reconcile such thoughts as he could, there was little doubt in which direction his speculations were leading him. 'Thought (or desires more properly) being hereditary it is difficult to imagine it anything but structure of brain hereditary,' he noted. Thought, morality, religiosity – all were cast into doubt by his evolving theory. 'Love of the deity effect of organization, oh you materialist!' he exclaimed.

Radical as his notebook speculations were over this period, it is important to emphasize that they did not constitute a complete renunciation of his Christian faith, still less a suppressed declaration of atheism. Darwin's faith might have been narrow and propositional, in a Paleyian kind of way, but his mind was extraordinarily broad and subtle. The notebooks reveal how he explored the impact of his theory on the potential concepts of God and of religion in a way that was constructive and nuanced, rather than dismissive or derogatory.

His attitude to special creation as compared to the law-governed evolution of life offers an example of this. Notebook B sees Darwin cast in an almost Newtonian role, articulating how the elegance of natural laws acting on creation would glorify rather than diminish God.

Astronomers might formerly have said that God ordered each planet to move in its particular destiny. — In same manner God orders each animal created with certain form in certain country, but how much more simple & sublime powers let attraction act according to certain law[s] [with] inevitable consequen[ces]. Let animals be created, then by the fixed laws of generation . . .

A similar point could be made regarding his thoughts about evolving religious sensibilities. Contemporaries might imagine God implanting an awareness of him within every human heart, but how much more elegant would it be if that awareness evolved naturally? The philosopher might say that 'the innate knowledge of creator has been implanted in us . . . by a separate act of God'. But how much more elegant would it be if that 'knowledge' were to have evolved in humanity like everything else? Why was it not 'a necessary integrant part of his most magnificent laws', laws that 'we profane in thinking not capable to produce every effect of every kind which surrounds us'. In such ways Darwin explored how his evolutionary theory might be accommodated with his religious thinking.

The fact was, however, that flexible as his mind was, transmutation was a fundamentally atheistic and anti-religious idea in the popular mind at the time. The establishment saw in transmutation a threat to the social and political order. It was the doctrine of radicals and revolutionaries, risking and sometimes losing their lives in their attempts to overthrow the status quo, not least the power of the established Church. If species could develop, change, evolve, become something they were not, so could men. The poor man was not made for his gate, any more than the rich man was for his castle. Evolution showed how fragile and mutable such estates were. When, in 1838, Darwin speculated about transmutation and materialism, he was whispering to himself 'the sort of flaming science [which] was favoured by street agitators, the people trying to overthrow the undemocratic state'.[114]

None of this made Darwin an atheist, but it did present him with an obvious category for his thinking. Darwin's problem was that he was such an innovative thinker. When he published his theory in 1859, prominent Christian thinkers like Charles Kingsley and Frederick Temple were able to accommodate its implications with Christianity. In the decades that followed, more and more were able to. But in 1838, when Darwin was speculating on these issues, there was no one else even vaguely orthodox who had considered them publicly. Transmutation, with its aura of materialism and determinism, was a non-religious, even an anti-religious idea. There was only one way Darwin could go.

From Paley to Malthus

On 28 September 1838, during the period of his most radical speculations, Darwin began to read the Revd Thomas Robert Malthus' *Essay on the Principle of Population*. A week later he had finished it. It was to rank as one of the most important books he ever read.

Malthus would have been familiar to Darwin. His essay had first appeared in 1798 and its ideas had been discussed widely, not least by both William Paley and Charles Lyell. Most noticeably, it was Malthus' thinking that had informed the controversial New Poor Law, which had been enacted when Darwin was on the *Beagle*. This replaced the ancient Elizabethan Poor Laws with a harsher regime in which the poor were forced to compete for work or enter the workhouse. Malthus died in 1834 but his legacy lived on.

His argument was comparatively simple. Population growth, he argued, 'is indefinitely greater than the power in the earth to produce subsistence for man'.[115] The natural tendency for a human population was to increase at a geometric rate, doubling every 25 years or so: 1, 2, 4, 8, 16, etc. The resources on which that population depended could increase 'only in an arithmetical ratio', however: 1, 2, 3, 4, 5, etc.

Something had to give and Malthus, unable to envisage how the agricultural or industrial revolutions might significantly improve resource availability, had no doubt what that would be. Population had to be checked. In 'plants and irrational animals' the equation was relatively straightforward. 'The power of increase is exerted; and the superabundant effects are repressed afterwards by want of room and nourishment.'[116]

In mankind, however, 'the effects of this check . . . are more complicated'. The urge to 'increase . . . his species' remained, as it did with 'irrational animals', powered by 'an equally powerful instinct'. However, here 'reason interrupts his career, and asks him whether he may not bring beings into the world, for whom he cannot provide the means of support'.[117] Mankind, in other words, is uniquely capable of understanding the problem.

That, however, made little difference. Reason might be able to identify the dilemma but it could do little to resolve it. If people listened to their reason and sought to minimize the number of their children, they would be led inexorably towards 'vice': contraception, abortion, infanticide. Only sexual abstinence or 'the restraint from marriage which is not followed by irregular gratifications' was a feasible option, and hardly a very realistic one.

If, on the other hand, people followed their instincts they would be led, equally certainly, towards misery. The population would be kept in check come whatever, and if people did not choose to do so themselves, 'nature' would do it for them. 'Severe labour and exposure to the seasons, extreme poverty, bad nursing of children, great towns, excesses of all kinds, the whole train of common diseases and epidemics, wars, plague, and famine': if humans didn't control their own population levels, these would. 'All these checks', Malthus concluded frankly, 'may be fairly resolved into misery and vice.'[118]

This was a grim vision of reality, a long way from Paley's 'happy world . . . [of] delighted existence'. It proved critical to the development of Darwin's theory, suggesting to him that it was nature – and a pitiless, unforgiving nature at that – which selected the fittest of one generation to breed the next. This was the keystone of his theory, intellectually elegant but morally ugly. Its implications can be traced through his notebooks and beyond.

In place of summer evenings crowded with 'myriads of happy beings', he now saw 'the dreadful but quiet war of organic beings, going on in the peaceful woods & smiling fields'. Humans were no different.

> When two races of men meet, they act precisely like two species of animals. — they fight, eat each other, bring diseases to each other &c., but then comes the most deadly struggle, namely which have the best fitted organization, or instincts.[119]

Darwin came across a pamphlet by Sir John Sebright about domestic breeding, which claimed that:

> A severe winter, or a scarcity of food, by destroying the weak and the unhealthy, has had all the good effects of the most skilful selection. In cold and barren countries no animals can live to the age of maturity, but those who have strong constitutions; the weak and the unhealthy do not live to propagate their infirmities.[120]

He scored the passage and remarked on its 'excellent observations of sickly offspring being cut off so that [they were] not propagated by nature'.

This was reality: an unsentimental vision of how grim life really was. It struck him deeply, occasioning one of his most famous aphorisms, in a letter to Joseph Hooker many years later. 'What a book a Devil's chaplain might write on the clumsy, wasteful, blundering low & horridly cruel works of nature!'[121]

And naturally, it made it into *The Origin of Species*.

> What war between insect and insect, between insects, snails, and other animals with birds and beasts of prey – all striving to increase, and all feeding on each other or on the trees or their seeds and seedlings, or on the other plants which first clothed the ground and thus checked the growth of the trees.[122]

Superficially this had nothing to do with his religious faith. Unlike his speculations on metaphysics and materialism, God rarely appears in these notes. In reality, however, it had profound implications for Darwin's beliefs. His theory not only did away with special creation, a tolerable loss, but, if Malthus was right, it also did away with the harmonious and beneficent creation of William Paley. Given how much store Paley and early nineteenth-century established religion put by this vision of happy, benign order, this was a serious challenge.

Similarly, re-evaluating the opening chapters of Genesis, so that they did not read like a bad scientific textbook, was easy. The geologists had been doing that for years. But integrating them with this brutal Malthusian vision of life, in which pain and suffering were *necessary* features of life rather than accidents resulting from an avoidable Fall, was more difficult.

Between the crises

Darwin's speculations over this period may not have razed his Christianity but they certainly severely eroded it. Although reported (by Edward Aveling) to have said in the last year of his life that, 'I never gave up Christianity until I was forty years of age,' his Christianity post-1839 was deeply hesitant and unsure.[123] The foundations of his supposed 'orthodoxy' on the *Beagle*, in particular the order and harmony of creation as articulated by William Paley, were either weakened or gone. Undoubtedly still theistic, and with genuine Christian leanings, the Darwin of the 1840s was only a Christian in the most tenuous sense.

His speculations continued after he married Emma in January 1839. His *Voyage of the Beagle* was published in May and he closed his last major notebook in June. He had 'a theory by which to work', although he was unsure what to do with it. Opposition to the New Poor Laws and popular Chartist demands for political and social reform did not comprise an auspicious background for publication. Any book, no matter how well researched, that established the theory of transmutation on a sound, scientific footing would have constituted a gentleman's suicide note. Emma was soon pregnant, giving birth to their first child, William Erasmus, in December 1839, and their second, Anne Elizabeth, in March 1841. London was becoming unsuitable for the growing Darwin clan, so they began house hunting. They chanced in July upon a former parsonage in Downe, Kent, and although Emma, pregnant again, was at first lukewarm, the family moved there in September.

By the time of the move, Darwin had put his theory on to paper. In May 1842 he, Emma and their young children had spent two months visiting their extended family in Maer and Shrewsbury. Darwin had taken this opportunity to write his first full explanation of his theory.

Darwin avoided religious controversy throughout his life. His interest in the subject was limited, his own ideas often unsure and in flux, and the advice of his father and people like Charles Lyell was for tact and silence. His 1842 sketch may not have been intended for publication but the same rules applied. Like *The Origin of Species* itself, the sketch for the most part circumvents religious or metaphysical questions.

Darwin did not avoid the topic altogether, however, alighting on it in an extended paragraph towards the end. In doing so he echoed many of the sentiments he had previously expressed in his notebooks. By comparison to special creation, evolution was an elegant and ingenious mechanism, and far better suited to any God worthy of the name.

It accords with what we know of the law impressed on matter by the Creator, that the creation and extinction of forms, like the birth and death of individuals should be the effect of secondary [laws] means.[124]

More than that, it was positively 'derogatory that the Creator of countless systems of worlds should have created each of the myriads of creeping parasites and worms which have swarmed each day of life on land and water on [this] one globe'.[125]

It may at first 'transcend our humble powers, to conceive laws capable of creating individual organisms, each characterized by the most exquisite workmanship and widely extended adaptations', but the existence of such laws was not only defensible but 'should exalt our notion of the power of the omniscient Creator'.[126]

'There is a simple grandeur in the view of life,' he continued, with words that passed largely unaltered into *The Origin of Species*,

> with its powers of growth, assimilation and reproduction, being originally breathed into matter under one or a few forms, and that whilst this our planet has gone circling on according to fixed laws, and land and water, in a cycle of change, have gone on replacing each other, that from so simple an origin, through the process of gradual selection of infinitesimal changes, endless forms most beautiful and most wonderful have been evolved.[127]

Such grandeur and beauty had a grave, if hidden cost, however. The ghost of Thomas Malthus was present at the banquet of life.

> We cease being astonished, however much we may deplore, that a group of animals should have been directly created to lay their eggs in bowels and flesh of other, – that some organisms should delight in cruelty, – that animals should be led away by false instincts, – that annually there should be an incalculable waste of eggs and pollen.[128]

The question was: Was it worth it? There was undoubtedly waste and pain, unavoidable and on an enormous scale. But could what resulted from that waste and pain ever justify or excuse it? Darwin's answer appeared to be a qualified 'yes'. 'From death, famine, rapine, and the concealed war of nature we can see that *the highest good, which we can conceive*, the creation of the higher animals has directly come.'[129]

That was the issue. If 'higher animals' – with all their splendour and sophistication, their grace and their grandeur, and ultimately their minds, metaphysics and morality – if they were indeed 'the highest good, which we can conceive' then maybe evolution by natural selection was not simply compatible with the goodness of God, such a Christian might recognize, but actively supportive of it. Everything hung on how the scales balanced between life's grandeur and its potential for grief.

Darwin followed his 1842 sketch with another, longer one two years later. And then he put both manuscripts away. His theory may not have been revolutionary or aggressively atheistic in his mind, but others would not have agreed with him.[130]

The Oracle of Reason, an illegal, atheistic penny paper, had been founded in 1841. It derided William Paley and his self-satisfied vision of life that the establishment used to justify itself. Materialism and evolution, of a self-creating, Lamarckian kind, were staple features. The editors attacked clerics and argued that had God existed, he would have planned 'less suffering and more enjoyment, less hypocrisy and more sincerity, fewer rapes, frauds, pious and impious butcheries'.[131]

Darwin shared neither the theological convictions nor the political ambitions of the *Oracle*'s editors. His was a scientific theory, not a scientific justification for a social revolution. He wanted to avoid being bracketed with such seditious, unscientific radicalism at all costs.

His instinct for caution was validated when, in October 1844, the publisher Robert Chambers anonymously published his book *Vestiges of the Natural History of Creation*. This presented to the world a comprehensive evolutionary view of creation, from astronomy to life to civilization. The book proved immensely popular but it and its author were instantly and savagely criticized by learned men for their scientific superficiality. 'Mr Vestiges' was pilloried as 'practical Atheist'. Darwin's geological educator, Adam Sedgwick, was particularly exercised. 'If the book be true, the labours of sober induction are in vain,' he wrote in the *Edinburgh Review*. 'Religion is a lie; human law is a mass of folly, and a base injustice; morality is moonshine; our labours for the black people of Africa were works of madmen; and man and woman are only better beasts!'[132] It was so bad, he said, that it could almost have been written by a woman.[133]

Darwin watched the storm from the protection of his family home at Downe. The reaction justified his decision not to publish. His theory was no *Vestiges*, but he did not want to take any risks. His attention turned to barnacles. In the ten years since he had returned from the *Beagle* he had worked furiously, analysing, writing, editing, revising and, above all, thinking his way through some uncharted and dangerous territories. Turning to a long and forensic study of barnacles, both living and fossilized, allowed him to re-immerse himself in his first loves: nature and experimentation.

Barnacles occupied much of the next eight years, a period that was regularly punctuated with bouts of ill-health. Darwin had first fallen seriously ill when on the *Beagle* in 1835, and had suffered again in 1838. It was only in the 1840s, however, that his health significantly deteriorated. He suffered from headaches, nausea, retching, acute vomiting and total debilitation. It was only periodic but sometimes the periods would last for months on end.

During one of these periods he started reading a number of books that indicate an ongoing interest in religious matters.[134] In April 1848, he opened *The Evidences of the Genuineness of the Gospels*, a two-volume tome by Andrews Norton, late professor of sacred studies at Harvard University, followed by Julius Hare's memoir of John Sterling and three books by Francis Newman, younger brother of John Henry Newman, who had recently been received into the Roman Catholic Church.

Norton was hostile to the critical scholarship that was emerging from Germany at the time, which was casting doubts over the historical reliability of both Testaments. The Gospels, he argued, had been ascribed to their correct authors and 'remain essentially the same as they were originally composed'. Perhaps surprisingly, Darwin marked the book as 'good'.

Julius Hare's memoir of John Sterling was less obviously ortho-dox. Sterling's life bore a curious resemblance to Darwin's. Born in 1806, he had attended Cambridge (without complet-ing his degree), been ordained, suffered from illness and then moved to London and the period of 'his greatest moral and intel-lectual energy'. There he read German biblical criticism, lost his Christian faith, and succumbed to the conviction that humans could never establish a 'deep and systematic knowledge on the laws and first principles of existence'. Shaken by close family deaths, he died in September 1844, saying that 'Christianity is a great comfort and blessing to me, although I am quite unable to believe all its original documents.' Darwin found the book 'modestly good'.

Francis Newman's three books were similarly unorthodox. Darwin began *The Soul* in September 1849. It was 'an impas-sioned plea for universal religion based on spiritual intuitions'. Its emphasis was on 'Awe, Wonder, [and] Admiration' leading to 'perceptions of Order, Design, Goodness and Wisdom', and thereafter to 'Reverence'. 'The only grounds for belief in a future life', according to Newman, lay in 'a full sympathy of our spirit with God's spirit'. Darwin left no comment on the book.

He started Newman's *History of the Hebrew Monarchy* in August 1850. The book, published anonymously, brought the full weight of German biblical scholarship to bear on the Old Testament history books, offering a radical new vision of

Hebrew history. Darwin thought it 'poor', although this was more likely to be because it assumed that 'the relations between the divine and the human mind [were] still substantially the same as ever'. His experiences and reflection on the Tierra del Fuego had convinced him that this could not be so.

Finally, in March 1851, he read Newman's spiritual autobiography, *Phases of Faith, or Passages from the History of my Creed*. This recounted Newman's journey from Calvinism, through Unitarianism to the fringes of religion. The book outlined Newman's intellectual and moral struggles with the Thirty-nine Articles, biblical authority, miracles, the doctrine of eternal damnation, and other orthodox subjects. Gradually Newman lost any distinctively Christian faith. Unlike John Sterling, however, he was not beset by disaffection. 'I felt no convulsion of mind, no emptiness of soul, no inward practical change,' he confessed. Darwin thought the book 'excellent'.

Darwin's brief notes on these books do not give any indication of whether and how they shaped his mind. For all Newman's and Sterling's lives might reflect his own, he seemed to like Andrews Norton's defence of the New Testament just as much as he disliked Newman's attack on the Old. All that can safely be said of his reading list is that it indicates an active interest in the possibility and nature of sincere religious belief even at this stage.

It hardly mattered, though, as something far more important was soon to happen to him.

No longer simply a theory

The problem of suffering had loomed large in Darwin's mind as he formulated his theory in the late 1830s. It was now to loom even larger in his life. Darwin's mother had died when he was just eight but the event seems to have left no lasting mark on him. Between her death and the 1840s he had lost no one to whom he had been close.

That changed shortly after the family arrived at Downe. Mary Eleanor, their third child, was born on 23 September 1842. She was a small and weak baby and lived only three weeks. Darwin's reaction is not recorded. Mary's death is not mentioned in any letters and merits the briefest mention in his personal journal: 'Mary Eleanor. Sept 23rd. born.— Ob[it]. October 16th.' Emma wrote to her sister-in-law, Fanny Wedgwood, a few days later, 'Our sorrow is nothing to what it would have been if she had lived longer and suffered more. Charles is well to-day and the funeral over, which he dreaded very much . . . '[135] Silence meant little. Charles and Emma clearly grieved at her death.

Mary's death turned out to be the first of a number of family losses. Emma's father, Josiah, had been bedridden for months and was in a very poor state of health. He died the following year. Her mother followed him two years later.

Darwin's own father was also declining. Darwin visited him in Shrewsbury in February and October 1847, and again in May 1848, acutely conscious of his failing health. Darwin's elder sisters, Susan and Catherine, nursed their father attentively and informed their brother of any changes. His death, although expected, was sudden and Darwin was unable to get to Shrewsbury in time.

Darwin was saddened rather than distraught. His father had been as overweight as his grandfather, but not as overbearing. Except for the tensions over his lack of ambition in the 1820s, their relationship had been good. His father had offered him advice, encouragement and largely unrestricted access to the family coffers. He had even backed down over the *Beagle* voyage, equipping and supporting him generously. Darwin's subsequent slow but steady progress in the world of scientific gentlemen had vindicated his father's trust. 'You were so beloved by him,' Catherine told her brother.[136] Their relationship had been as close as any of two men of their age and class could have been.

Darwin missed the funeral, although seemingly more by accident than design. This dereliction of duty remained with him, however, and when his cousin William Fox found himself in precisely the same situation, he wrote sympathetically:

> I grieve to hear that your health prevents you attending the Funeral: this was my case, & though it is only a ceremony I felt deeply grieved at this deprivation & you no doubt will feel this more.[137]

Darwin was writing to Fox on 27 March 1851, from Malvern, where he had brought his daughter Annie. Darwin had suffered his mysterious nausea and acute vomiting for years, but his condition had recently deteriorated, his symptoms worsening after his father's death. He began to keep a health diary in January 1849 and sought conventional medical advice from experts, such as Henry Holland, a respected London doctor and a Darwin cousin. When this failed, he looked elsewhere, and alighted upon 'hydropathy' or water treatment. This had become fashionable in the 1840s and Fox had visited and recommended Dr James Gully and his respectable establishment in Malvern.

Darwin read Gully's book and decided to take the plunge, carting the entire Darwin household – Emma, William, Anne, Henrietta, George, Elizabeth, Francis, their maids, the governess and the butler – there in March 1849. They remained for three months although, for Darwin at least, it was no holiday. His routine was a tough one. He woke at 6.45 and was 'scrubbed with rough towel in cold water for 2 or 3 minutes, which . . . makes me very like a lobster'. He then wore a compress, 'dipt in cold water every 2 hours . . . all day'. Midday saw him putting his feet 'in cold water with a little mustard', where 'they are violently rubbed . . . for 10 minutes'. 'The coldness makes my feet ache much,' he complained. There was more cold water at five o'clock. The routine was punctuated only by regular walks, rest and horribly plain food. 'At no time must I take any sugar, butter, spices, tea, bacon or anything good,' he lamented.

Unpleasant as it was, the routine appeared to work. 'I have had much sickness this week, but certainly I have felt much stronger & the sickness has depressed me much less,' he wrote to Susan.[138]

So persuaded was he of the benefits of Dr Gully's water treatment, he suggested taking Annie there in 1851. Charles and Emma now had three daughters, Annie, Henrietta (Etty) and Elizabeth (Bessy), the latter two being born in 1843 and 1847 respectively. All three girls had been ill with scarlet fever in 1849 and Annie had never fully recovered.

Annie was a buoyant but affectionate and sensitive girl, 'cordial, frank, open . . . without any shade of reserve', and devoted to her father. She was a special favourite of his. Darwin was worried about the long-term effects of her scarlet fever and also feared that she had inherited his 'wretched digestion'. Her health deteriorated in June 1850 and Darwin took her (and the family) on a brief therapeutic holiday to Ramsgate in October that year.

This proved ineffective and Annie's health worsened so, in March 1851, shortly after her tenth birthday, Darwin took her to Dr Gully. Father and daughter were accompanied by Annie's nurse, her governess and her sister Henrietta. Darwin stayed with the party until 28 March, when he returned to London and then to Downe. Gully's hydropathy had done him a great deal of good and he had no doubt Annie would benefit too.

A fortnight later he got an urgent message. Annie had taken a turn for the worse and was vomiting badly. Darwin rushed back, arriving in Malvern on Maundy Thursday, 17 April. Annie looked wretched, although she did at least recognize her father when he arrived. Dr Gully had 87 other patients and could not spare the Darwins much time. Still, he assured Darwin, Annie was 'several degrees better' than she had been. 'Dr Gully is most confident there is strong hope,' Darwin reassured Emma later that day.[139]

Annie's condition worsened in the night. Her pulse became irregular and she slipped into semi-consciousness. It was 'from hour to hour a struggle between life & death'.[140] Gully believed she was dying and stayed with Charles all night. Somehow, she survived. She vomited at 6 a.m. and then again throughout the day, unable to keep down the thin gruel she was fed.

Darwin tried to shield Emma, shortly expecting her eighth child, from Annie's pain: 'She does not suffer thank God.' He could not, however, disguise his own. 'It is much bitterer & harder to bear than I expected – Your note made me cry much – but I must not give way & can avoid doing so, by not thinking about her.'

She suffered through Good Friday. 'Her one good point is her pulse, now regular & not very weak,' Darwin recorded at midday. 'Excepting for this there would be no hope.' 'She keeps the same,' he wrote three hours later. 'We must hope against hope.' [141]

He dispatched the letter and immediately began another. The news was little better. Darwin searched for grains of hope. 'She appears dreadfully exhausted, & I thought for some time she was sinking, but she has now rallied a little,' he wrote in the early evening. And then, at 7.30: 'Dr Gully has been & thank God he says though the appearances are so bad, positively no one important symptom is worse, & that he yet has hopes— positively he has Hopes.' 'Oh my dear be thankful,' he exclaimed.[142]

Friday night was better. Annie slept 'tranquilly . . . through-out the whole night'. At one point she said 'Papa' 'quite distinctly', although by now he hardly knew her. 'You would not in the least recognize her,' he told Emma, 'with her poor hard, sharp pinched features; I could only bear to look at her by forgetting our former dear Annie. There is nothing in common between the two.'[143]

Despite everything, things began to look up. Dr Gully came to see her and, noticing how peacefully she slept, told Darwin 'she is turning the corner'. So it seemed. She sat up and took 'two spoonfuls of tea with evident relish, and no sickness'.

Darwin was almost delirious with joy. 'I then dared picture to myself my own former Annie with her dear affectionate radiant face.'[144] 'What happiness! How I do thank God!' Emma replied.[145]

Gully visited again late Saturday night, telling Charles: 'I can give no reason for my intuition, but yet I think she will recover.' Darwin sat by her bedside through Saturday night watching over her as she slept peacefully. He kept Emma informed hourly, confessing, 'It is a relief to me to tell you: for whilst writing to you, I can cry; tranquilly.'

She vomited again, badly, on Easter Sunday morning. Her bladder was now paralysed and a catheter had to be inserted. In spite of this, the signs were still deemed positive. Mr Coates, the medical officer, took her pulse and immediately said, 'I declare I almost think she will recover.' Recent fevers such as the one Annie was experiencing, he explained, often appeared very bad but had tended not to be fatal. 'Oh my dear was not this joyous to hear,' Darwin wrote at 10 a.m.

Her condition picked up throughout the morning. Her senses recovered and she called for him again. Darwin's spirits rose higher but he was by now completely exhausted. 'These alternations of no hope & hope sicken one's soul,' he told Emma.[146]

The emotional rollercoaster continued into Monday. Annie emptied her own bladder and bowels for the first time in over a week, which Darwin judged 'very good'. Desperate for encouragement, he thought again of the little girl he loved so dearly.

> An hour ago I was foolish with delight & pictured her to myself making custards (whirling round) as, I think, she called them. I told her I thought she would be better & she so meekly said 'thank you'. Her gentleness is inexpressibly touching.[147]

Darwin seized on any sign of recovery.

She asked for orange this morning, the first time she has asked
for anything except water . . . Fanny gave her a spoonful of tea
a little while ago, & asked her whether it was good & she cried
out quite audibly 'it is beautifully good'.[148]

In spite of such signs, her conditioned worsened on Tues-
day. Diarrhoea set in. Darwin could hardly take any more and
his own stomach troubles erupted. Annie was sinking, slipping
into unconsciousness. 'Twice amid her wanderings she made
pathetic attempts to sing.'[149] By Wednesday morning her
breathing was shallow, her body wasted. Eventually, she died at
midday.

'Our poor dear dear child . . . went to her final sleep most
tranquilly, most sweetly,' he wrote to Emma later in the day.
'She expired without a sigh.' The memory of her was almost
too painful to recall. 'How desolate it makes one to think of
her frank cordial manners . . . I cannot remember ever seeing
the dear child naughty. God bless her.'[150] Gully's death
certificate recorded 'bilious fever with typhoid character'.

Annie's death devastated Darwin. 'She was my favourite
child,' he told Fox frankly. 'Her cordiality, openness, buoyant
joyousness & strong affection made her most loveable. Poor dear
little soul.'[151]

A week after her death, Darwin recorded his memories of
her, hoping to capture her 'strong affection' and 'buoyant
joyousness' before they faded from his mind. He owned a
daguerreotype which was 'very like her', but it was already two
years out of date and failed entirely to capture the character of
the daughter he had lost.[152]

Darwin's overriding memory was of her 'joyousness'. She was
a young and feminine girl whose 'every movement [was] elastic
& full of life & vigour'. She was trustworthy, generous, sensitive
and affectionate. 'She liked being kissed; indeed every expression in her countenance beamed with affection & kindness.'

Darwin remembered how she pirouetted before him as they walked round the garden at home; how 'she would spend hours in comparing the colours of any objects with a book of mine'; how 'she used sometimes to come running down stairs with a stolen pinch of snuff for me'; how 'she would at almost anytime spend half-an-hour in arranging my hair, "making it" as she called it "beautiful".'

And he remembered her final, debilitating illness.

> She never once complained; never became fretful; was ever considerate of others; & was thankful in the most gentle, pathetic manner for everything done for her. When so exhausted that she could hardly speak, she praised everything that was given her, & said some tea 'was beautifully good'.

She was to be 'the solace of our old age'. 'I always thought, that come what might, we should have had in our old age, at least one loving soul, which nothing could have changed.' It was not to be.

'She must have known how we loved her,' he concluded. 'Oh that she could now know how deeply, how tenderly we do still & shall ever love her dear joyous face.'

Annie was not the first child Darwin lost, nor the last. But nothing was the same after she died. Nearly a decade later, in September 1860, he wrote to his friend Thomas Huxley, whose four-year-old son had just died of scarlet fever.

> I know well how intolerable is the bitterness of such grief. Yet believe me, that time, & time alone, acts wonderfully. To this day, though so many years have passed away, I cannot think of one child without tears rising in my eyes; but the grief is become tenderer & I can even call up the smile of our lost darling, with something like pleasure.[153]

Emma grieved too. Her daughter Henrietta later wrote that 'my mother never really recovered from this grief. She very rarely spoke of Annie, but when she did the sense of loss was always there unhealed.' But for Charles, lacking Emma's faith, alert to the seeming inevitability of suffering according to his theory and having witnessed every moment of his daughter's agonizing and degrading death, Annie's loss was simply unbearable. 'My father could not bear to reopen his sorrow, and he never, to my knowledge, spoke of her,' Henrietta wrote.[154]

The *Beagle* had opened up a new world and new thoughts for Darwin. These had begun to erode the foundations of his narrowly Paleyian, 'orthodox' Christian faith. The subsequent years of speculation saw that faith profoundly destabilized. Darwin had searched for accommodations, if not with his previous 'orthodoxy' at least with a concept of God that was intellectually tenable and Christian, at least in outline. He alighted on some but they were in uncharted territory – indeed, territory that was deemed largely atheistic in the popular mind – and they failed to answer his questions convincingly. 'The creation of the higher animals' was undoubtedly a supreme good, but if, as his notebooks speculated, even the highest of those higher animals was little more than a civilized orang-utan, was that supreme good actually worth the incalculable pain and suffering?

The theoretical answer was yes. But then, in the Malvern Hills, he experienced the reality, and it changed his mind. Darwin, as we shall see, remained a theist for years, and even in his moments of severest doubt never considered himself an atheist. But the last remnants of his belief in the good, personal, just, loving God of Christianity died, at Easter 1851, with his dearly beloved daughter.

3

'The problem insoluble': doubts that remained

------◆◆◆◆------

Darwin's religious journey did not end in 1851 but it did change course irrevocably. The last three decades of his life saw him rise to international prominence and publish some of the most influential scientific books of all time. They saw him caught in a maelstrom of public debate, albeit at a distance, much of which was about an issue on which he had not published a single word. And they also saw him write more, and more frankly, about that issue, albeit in private, than he had at any time before Annie's death.

Darwin's increased willingness to discuss his religious beliefs is explained partly by society's gradual opening up to the possibility of doubt and unorthodoxy and partly by the publication of his theory of evolution in 1859. Such questions were out in public now and could be discussed in a way that was impossible in the 1830s and 40s – although that did not, of course, mean the theory or its implications were uncontroversial.

Beyond these basic social changes, however, there is a sense in which Darwin could speak more openly on the subject because it no longer mattered so much to him. Darwin wasn't sure what he believed – indeed he became less sure as the years went on – but he was sure what he didn't believe. In his experience, the universe was neither moral nor just. Dearly loved children died in it, for no reason other than that they were weak and vulnerable. This did not disprove the existence of God, of course, but the only God it left room for was one who didn't, at least in human terms, *matter* very much. After Annie, Darwin could speculate, sometimes at length, on the possibility of God because, now, there simply wasn't as much riding on it.

The Origin of Species

Following Annie's death, Darwin went back to his barnacles. He continued dissecting, thinking and writing about them for the next two years, an effort that earned him the Royal Society's prestigious Royal Medal in 1853.

Barnacles had removed him from his evolutionary theory, at least directly, for nearly eight years but, in 1854, he returned to work on it. At first he read and corresponded widely, and experimented on seeds, but in May 1856, on the advice of Charles Lyell, he put pen to paper again, this time with the intention, as he told Fox, of making 'my Book as perfect as ever I can'.[155]

He was about halfway through it when he received a letter from Alfred Russel Wallace, a naturalist who had been collecting specimens in the Far East. Darwin had written to Wallace in December 1855 to request skins of foreign breeds of domestic fowl, and then again in May 1857, asking for facts relating to the 'means of distribution of all organic beings found on oceanic islands'.[156]

A year later Wallace shocked Darwin by sending him the manuscript of a paper entitled, 'On the tendency of varieties to depart indefinitely from the original type'. Darwin was devastated. 'I never saw a more striking coincidence. If Wallace had my M.S. sketch written out in 1842 he could not have made a better short abstract!' he wrote to Lyell.[157]

Wallace had written to Darwin asking him whether he thought his paper sufficiently important to send to Lyell, who had responded positively to one of Wallace's former papers.

Darwin knew that Lyell would indeed appreciate the idea. Moreover, he felt duty bound to write to Wallace, offering to send his paper to a journal for publication. 'So all my originality, whatever it may amount to, will be smashed,' he lamented.[158]

He consulted with his friends Lyell and Hooker, who were aware of Darwin's ever-expanding species manuscript and were as loath as he was to see him to lose credit for his life's work. They recognized his duty to send Wallace's manuscript for publication but suggested instead that Darwin work up an abstract of his idea and that both papers might be published simultaneously. Darwin was nervous about the arrangement, writing that 'I would far rather burn my whole book than that he or any man should think that I had behaved in a paltry spirit.'[159] Eventually, however, he acquiesced.

As it happened, Darwin already had just such an abstract in the form of a letter he had sent to Asa Gray, professor of natural history at Harvard University, a year or so earlier. So it was that the theory of evolution by natural selection was launched upon the world at a meeting of the Linnean Society on 1 July 1858, in the form of two papers: the one that Wallace had sent to Darwin, and one of Darwin's own, 'On the Tendency of Species to form Varieties; and on the Perpetuation of Varieties and Species by Natural Means of Selection'.

Darwin's stomach and nerves would normally have deterred him from attending in any case, but two days beforehand he lost another child, Charles Waring. He was two years old. 'I hope to God he did not suffer so much as he appeared,' Darwin wrote to Hooker. 'It was the most blessed relief to see his poor little innocent face resume its sweet expression in the sleep of death – Thank God he will never suffer more in this world.'[160]

The Linnean papers were received with surprisingly little excitement, and Darwin set to work immediately writing *The Origin of Species*. Twenty years later the botanist Henry Ridley wrote to Darwin about a sermon that Edward Pusey, a prominent Oxford clergyman and Hebrew scholar, had delivered. Pusey had claimed that Darwin had written *The Origin* 'with a Quasi Theological not with a scientific object', his intention being 'to overthrow the dogma of separate creations'. The result, he claimed, was that Darwin had been 'biased when [he] wrote it & the result is therefore invalid'.[161]

In customary fashion Darwin was not drawn by Pusey's accusations, telling Ridley that the sermon 'did not seem to me worthy of any attention'. He did, however, inform Ridley that 'Dr Pusey was mistaken in imagining that I wrote the Origin with any relation whatever to Theology'.[162]

Darwin was undoubtedly right in his recollections. He eschewed religious controversy wherever possible. He had advised Wallace to 'avoid [the] whole subject [of man]' in one of his papers as, although 'it is the highest & most interesting problem for the naturalist', it is also 'surrounded with prejudices'.[163] He practised what he preached. Mankind was largely absent from *The Origin*, as he was from the 1842 and 1844 sketches.

In spite of its author's meticulous circumspection, when the book was published its implications for human beings were clear to all and provoked a range of strong reactions. These were by no means easily divisible into religious hostility and scientific acceptance. Some leading churchmen, such as Samuel Wilberforce, the Bishop of Oxford, were hostile; others like Frederick Temple, future Archbishop of Canterbury, wholly encouraging. Some prominent scientists, not least Darwin's leading advocates – Gray, Huxley and Hooker – were (critically) supportive; others, like Sir John Herschel, lukewarm at best; and still others like Louis Agassiz, professor of natural history at Harvard, or Richard Owen, Britain's leading comparative anatomist, were severely critical. Nor was it always easy to tell which way a newspaper or journal would jump. The *Rambler*, a liberal Catholic journal, was severely critical, while the *English Churchman* was rather less so.[164]

Interestingly, one of the earliest applications of the theory, even before *The Origin* was published, came from a clergyman, the Revd Henry Baker Tristram, who in 1859 published an article on North African ornithology in *Ibis*, the international journal of avian science. Tristram 'was convinced of the truth of the views set forth by Messrs. Darwin and Wallace [in their Linnean Society Lecture]', and went on to say that:

> Knowing that *God* ordinarily works by natural means, it might be the presumption of an unnecessary miracle to assume a distinct and separate origin for many of those which we term species ... Every peculiarity of difference in the living inhabitants of each country is admirably adapted by the wisdom of their beneficent Creator for the support and preservation of the species.[165]

It was an argument that later gained much ground among Christian thinkers, although one that Tristram himself later distanced himself from as he began to turn against the theory.

Regarding personal reactions, Darwin was most stung by that of Adam Sedgwick, his old teacher and professor, now aged 74 but still lecturing undergraduates and still very Paleyian in his mindset. Sedgwick wrote to thank Darwin for his advance copy but confided that he had read it 'with more pain than pleasure'.[166]

He criticised it for 'desert[ing ... the] tram-road of all solid physical truth' in favour of speculation and 'assumptions which can neither be proved nor disproved'. Such scientific criticism was earnest but there was no disguising the real source of his antipathy. 'Passages in your book ... greatly shocked my moral taste,' he said, not least its apparent materialism.

77

There is a moral or metaphysical part of nature as well as a physical. A man who denies this is deep in the mire of folly . . . Were it possible (which thank God it is not) to break [the link between material and moral], humanity in my mind, would suffer a damage that might brutalize it—& sink the human race into a lower grade of degradation than any into which it has fallen since its written records tell us of its history.

The theory was also criticised by the erstwhile captain of the *Beagle*, Robert FitzRoy, who had written to *The Times*, signing himself 'Senex'. Darwin guessed the author's identity but was not unduly alarmed. He esteemed FitzRoy's opinion rather less than Sedgwick's. 'It is a pity he did not add his theory of the extinction of Mastodon &c from the door of the ark being made too small,' he wrote to Lyell. 'What a mixture of conceit & folly.'[167]

Other reactions were more positive. One of the warmest letters Darwin received was from the author and clergyman Charles Kingsley, shortly to become professor of modern history at Cambridge. 'All I have seen of it awes me,' he gushed. 'If you be right,' he said, 'I must give up much that I have believed & written.'[168]

This was no painful loss of faith, however. Rather, Kingsley saw his Christian faith evolving, being transformed, and for the better.

From two common superstitions, at least, I shall be free . . . 1) I have long since, from watching the crossing of domesticated animals & plants, learnt to disbelieve the dogma of the permanence of species. 2) I have gradually learnt to see that it is just as noble a conception of Deity, to believe that he created primal forms capable of self development into all forms needful pro tempore & pro loco, as to believe that He required a fresh act of intervention to supply the lacunas wh[ich] he himself had made.

Kingsley was speculating in a fashion not dissimilar to the way in which Darwin had when exploring the possibilities of religious accommodation in his notebooks 20 years earlier. His words so impressed Darwin that he included them anonymously in the second edition of *The Origin*, published in January 1860.

Darwin saw in Kingsley's letter a way of obviating the religious criticism and controversy that were gathering around the book. In Janet Browne's words, these were 'conciliatory words that Darwin would otherwise never have allowed and certainly did not deliver in his own voice'.[169] Although there is undoubtedly some truth in this, it is unlikely to be the whole truth.

The first edition of *The Origin* contained two epigraphs.[170] Both were about God, and both would have been happily countersigned by Kingsley. Indeed, the former was all but a paraphrase of Kingsley's own sentiments. It came from one of the Bridgewater Treatises, a series of tracts commissioned by the Earl of Bridgewater to explore 'the Power, Wisdom, and Goodness of God, as manifested in the Creation'.

Darwin's quotation came from the third treatise, on *Astronomy and General Physics*, by William Whewell, former professor of moral philosophy at Cambridge.

> But with regard to the material world, we can at least go so far as this—we can perceive that events are brought about not by insulated interpositions of Divine power, exerted in each particular case, but by the establishment of general laws.

The second was from Francis Bacon's *Advancement of Learning*, written 250 years earlier. This was, again, something of a sop to religious sensibilities. But it also expressed a sentiment that was close to Darwin's heart, one to which he would return in later life: the idea that 'God's word' and 'God's works' were both legitimate and *separate* disciplines.

To conclude, therefore, let no man out of a weak conceit of
sobriety, or an ill-applied moderation, think or maintain, that
a man can search too far or be too well studied in the book of
God's word, or in the book of God's works; divinity or philosophy; but rather let men endeavour an endless progress or
proficience in both.

To these, Darwin appended a third epigraph in the second
edition of the book.[171] This was from *The Analogy of Religion*
by Joseph Butler, an early eighteenth-century English bishop,
which argued that it was as legitimate to see God in 'natural'
processes as it was to detect him in 'supernatural' interruptions
to those processes.

The only distinct meaning of the word 'natural' is stated,
fixed, or settled; since what is natural as much requires and
presupposes an intelligent agent to render it so, i.e. to effect
it continually or at stated times, as what is supernatural or
miraculous does to effect it for once.

Once again, this epigraph can be understood as a means of
heading off 'orthodox' criticism at the pass. Before they even
got to the book, hostile readers, wedded to special creation, would
read about how God could be just as present in and through
natural, everyday phenomena as through supernatural ones.
Nor was such an argument particularly new or innovative.
In one form or another it can be traced right back to both
the New and Old Testaments, which 'frequently depict divine
communication or disclosure as taking place within the realm
of nature, being mediated through natural processes, events
and entities'.[172] The irony is that, biblically orthodox as this
view was, it was deemed unorthodox or at least unusual at
the time.

Darwin also made several other additions to the second edition of *The Origin*, which he subsequently came openly to regret.

Although he frequently used the words 'create', 'created',
'creating' in the first edition of *The Origin*, Darwin used the

word 'creator' only sparingly and even then usually to convey others' views (for example, 'He who believes in separate and innumerable acts of creation will say that in these cases it has pleased the Creator to cause a being of one type to take the place of one of another type'[173]). Towards the end of the book, however, Darwin used the word in a clearly personal way:

> To my mind it accords better with what we know of the laws impressed on matter by the Creator, that the production and extinction of the past and present inhabitants of the world should have been due to secondary causes, like those determining the birth and death of the individual.[174]

The idea clearly echoes the Whewell and Butler epigraphs, and indeed Kingsley's sentiments. Darwin is certainly not confessing anything like orthodox Christian faith here. Rather his conclusion and the epigraphs he chose for the book describe well the blurred theism that characterized his mind at the time.

The same cannot be said of the second edition of *The Origin* in which Darwin made moves, albeit very minor ones, towards more personal and obviously religious language. This happened in two places. First, he added the phrase: 'I should infer from analogy that probably all the organic beings which have ever lived on this earth have descended from some one primordial form, into which life was first breathed by the Creator.'[175] Second, he changed the book's iconic concluding sentence. Where the first edition had read: 'There is grandeur in this view of life, with its several powers, having been originally breathed into a few forms or into one...', the second now read: 'There is grandeur in this view of life, with its several powers, having been originally breathed by the Creator into a few forms or into one...'[176]

Darwin came to regret these insertions, removing the former although not the latter from subsequent editions, and commenting to Hooker, 'I have long regretted that I truckled to public opinion & used [the] Pentateuchal term of creation, by which I really meant "appeared" by some wholly unknown process.'[177]

His frustration was not because he had subsequently developed a well-formed idea about how life on earth had originated. He hadn't. Rather, he disliked blurring the lines between scientific and theological terms, a point he made in response to an *Athenæum* review of the book:

> Your reviewer sneers with justice at my use of the 'Pentateuchal terms' 'of one primordial form into which life was first breathed.' In a purely scientific work I ought perhaps not to have used such terms.[178]

Darwin was keen to avoid controversy but not at any cost, and certainly not at the cost of weakening the scientific integrity of his theory. He was happy with the epigraphs he chose, his sparing references to the creator, and his addition of Kingsley's letter to subsequent editions of the book. But his theory was scientific, standing or falling on those credentials alone, and he wanted to avoid anything that detracted from that.

Although the publication of *The Origin of Species* marked a sea-change in the story of Victorian faith and doubt, it marked no such change in Darwin's own story. It preserved, more or less intact, much of what he had first articulated in his species sketches nearly 20 years earlier. It was not written in an atheistic mindset, nor to promote such a mindset. 'I had no intention to write atheistically,' Darwin told his friend Asa Gray.[179]

Indeed, *The Origin* was deliberately constructed so as to *permit* the accommodation of his theory within a (nuanced) understanding of the Christian faith. 'I see no good reason why the views given in this volume should shock the religious feelings of any one,' Darwin wrote explicitly in the second and subsequent editions of the book.[180]

That openness to accommodation was driven not so much by Darwin's own equivocal theism as by his desire to minimize hostility to his theory from the religious establishment. That recognized, Darwin was never a dissembler and it is highly unlikely that he would have included and *kept* the epigraphs or, indeed, Kingsley's comments, had they not resonated with his own thinking.

This is not to claim that Darwin remained a closet Christian into the 1860s. He did not. It is, however, to confirm what Darwin says explicitly in his autobiography: that at the time of *The Origin*'s publication he not only thought it was entirely possible to accept both God and evolution by natural selection, but he assumed that position himself.

Design, suffering and happiness

Darwin may have been a theist at the time of *The Origin*, but the position caused him some discomfort. He was sure that it was possible to accommodate religious faith with his theory, a view he held right up to the end of his life, telling one correspondent, John Fordyce, in 1879 that, 'it seems to me absurd to doubt that a man may be an ardent Theist & an evolutionist'.[181] He did, however, recognize some tension in that accommodation, a tension that is clearest in some of his post-*Origin* correspondence, not least with Asa Gray.[182]

Darwin was first introduced to Gray in 1839, by their mutual friend, Joseph Hooker. At the time Gray was a young professor at the new University of Michigan, but his brilliance was already earning him recognition and three years later he became professor of natural history at Harvard University, a post he held for the next 46 years. He was later to become president of the American Academy of Arts and Sciences and president of the American Association for the Advancement of Science. More than anyone else, Gray was responsible for the promotion and success of Darwin's theory in America, arranging for its publication there. 'Asa Gray is fighting admirably in U[nited] States. He is thorough master of subject,' Darwin wrote to Huxley in 1860.[183]

He was also a devout and thoughtful Christian, with a background in 'New School' Presbyterianism. He later described himself as 'one who is scientifically, and in his own fashion, a Darwinian, philosophically a convinced theist, and religiously an acceptor of the "creed commonly called the Nicene," as the exponent of the Christian faith'.[184]

Darwin and Gray shared a close friendship as well as professional interests, and corresponded frequently and at length. Darwin had informed Gray of his theory years before its publication, and it was an abstract of the idea that Darwin had sent to Gray that formed the basis of his paper at the Linnean Society in 1858.

The Origin was as controversial in the United States as in Britain, with the added factor that Louis Agassiz, the most highly respected scientist of the day, was actively hostile. 'Agassiz ... has been helping the circulation of [*The Origin*] by denouncing it as atheistical,' Gray informed Darwin.[185] Improved circulation or not, Darwin was having none of it. 'Certainly I agree with you', he replied to Gray, 'that my views are not at all necessarily atheistical.'[186]

That said, he did not share Gray's personal beliefs nor his reasons for holding them. In particular, the two men disagreed on the evidence (or lack of it) for design within the process of natural selection. It formed the basis of what Darwin described as a 'quasi-theological controversy' that he had with both Gray and Charles Lyell.[187]

The debate was seemingly about design, although it soon moved to a cluster of other related issues, such as suffering, moral order, justice, free will and God's omnipotence and omniscience. Gray, like Charles Lyell, argued that 'variation has been led along certain beneficial lines', the process of evolution being actively guided by God.[188]

Darwin could not accept this. On the surface, this was because of suffering. If God had been leading evolution through a series of providential variations, surely he would have done so in a more benevolent way?

> I cannot see, as plainly as others do, & as I should wish to do, evidence of design & beneficence on all sides of us. There seems to me too much misery in the world. I cannot persuade myself that a beneficent & *omnipotent* God would have designedly created the Ichneumonidæ with the express intention of their feeding within the living bodies of caterpillars, or that a cat should play with mice.[189]

Convinced as Darwin sounds here, suffering was not, in theory at least, a knock-down argument for him. Most of his other ruminations on the question, while acknowledging the ubiquity and severity of suffering, sounded a rather different note. In his only explicit reference to William Paley in *The Origin of Species*, Darwin had written:

> Natural selection will never produce in a being anything injurious to itself, for natural selection acts solely by and for the good of each. No organ will be formed, as Paley has remarked, for the purpose of causing pain or for doing an injury to its possessor.[190]

Similarly, when addressing the question of suffering and happiness in his autobiography, at some length, he again struck a note significantly different from that in his letter to Gray.

> Some writers indeed are so much impressed with the amount of suffering in the world, that they doubt, if we look to all sentient beings, whether there is more of misery or of happiness;— whether the world as a whole is a good or a bad one. According to my judgment happiness decidedly prevails.[191]

This wasn't sentimentality. Darwin's justification was rooted in his own theory.

> If the truth of this conclusion be granted, it harmonises well with the effects which we might expect from natural selection. If all

the individuals of any species were habitually to suffer to an extreme degree they would neglect to propagate their kind; but we have no reason to believe that this has ever or at least often occurred. Some other considerations, moreover, lead to the belief that all sentient beings have been formed so as to enjoy, as a general rule, happiness.[192]

Darwin acknowledges that 'this would be very difficult to prove', but is resolute on the issue.

The sum of such pleasures as these, which are habitual or frequently recurrent, give, as I can hardly doubt, to most sentient beings an excess of happiness over misery, although many occasionally suffer much.[193]

In articulating this opinion, in his autobiography written in the 1870s, Darwin is back in the territory of his first full-length evolutionary sketch over 30 years earlier. The answer to that key question – Is the suffering worth it? – depends, on the one hand, on what you judge 'it' to be and how highly you value it, and on the other, how much suffering there is to account for.

Darwin's answer in 1842 was a *tentative* 'yes'. 'The creation of the higher animals' was sufficiently wonderful – 'the highest good [of] which we can conceive' – to make natural selection a legitimate means of getting there. This wasn't to ignore or downplay the reality or enormity of suffering. Rather it was to consider it alongside and in the light of life's grandeur. It was, in essence, to hear both sides of the argument and make a balanced, if cautious, decision for one of them.

Thirty years later, and in spite of everything that had happened since, his answer – at least his *theoretical* answer – remained 'yes'. The suffering was great, but on balance 'happiness decidedly prevails'.

It is worth noting, just as an aside, that such calculations apparently informed Darwin's mind more broadly in his correspondence with Gray. Gray and Darwin wrote to each other for years, but their 'quasi-theological' debate was concentrated in the early 1860s, coinciding with the start of the American Civil War. This was to become a point of tension between them, with Darwin's hatred of slavery blinding him to some of the political details to which Gray was more alert. 'Great God how I should like to see that greatest curse on Earth Slavery abolished,' Darwin exclaimed to Gray in June 1861.[194] Gray was no supporter of slavery but nor did he relish the prospect of seeing his country torn apart and his countrymen killed. Darwin felt no such reserve.

> Some few, & I am one, even wish to *God*, though at the loss of millions of lives, that the North would proclaim a crusade against *Slavery*. In the long run, a million horrid deaths would be amply repaid in the cause of humanity.[195]

It is an extraordinary sentiment, not least from one so sensitive to pain and suffering. It shows how Darwin's passionate abolitionism survived well into middle age. But it is more interesting for coming in the midst of a debate about the nature and morality of natural selection. The abolition of slavery was, for Darwin, the 'highest good'. It was so high, in fact, that it would justify 'a million horrid deaths'. Sometimes, when the outcome was sufficiently good, extensive pain and suffering were, apparently, justifiable.

God in evolution

'Happiness decidedly prevail[ing]' was not necessarily enough, though. It was one thing to believe that happiness outweighed suffering in the natural world, but it was quite another to say that this balance, or indeed any suffering, could be reconciled with the existence of any God worth the name. It was, in effect, a theological rather than a biological question.

Darwin was clear where he stood on this in his autobiography. Although 'some have attempted to explain [suffering] in reference to man by imagining that it serves for his moral improvement', even if one accepted this argument, it says nothing about the pain of animals. 'The number of men in the world is as nothing compared with that of all other sentient beings, and these often suffer greatly without any moral improvement.'

'A being so powerful and so full of knowledge as a God who could create the universe, is to our finite minds omnipotent and omniscient,' Darwin reasoned, 'and it revolts our understanding to suppose that his benevolence is not unbounded, for what advantage can there be in the sufferings of millions of the lower animals throughout almost endless time?'[196]

This, Darwin acknowledged, was a 'very old argument' but it remained a powerful one, refined by his own theory. If God was omnipotent but sentient creatures suffered in the way they did, what role could or did he play vis-à-vis natural selection?

This was the question he explored at length with Asa Gray and Charles Lyell, both of whom ascribed to God an active role in the process of evolution. In discussing the question with his two friends, Darwin found himself edging out of his comfort zone and into metaphysics, and he repeatedly claimed that he was in a 'muddle' and that 'such question[s are] beyond the human intellect, like "predestination & free will" or "the origin of evil"'.[197] In reality, such questions were not so much 'like' predestination and free will as actually about predestination and free will.

Gray and Lyell saw in natural selection a 'higher law of providential arrangement', which involved more than establishing a process that would, given sufficient time, result in life that was complex, sentient and ultimately moral. Rather, their creator seemed more hands-on, actively leading evolution on, acting as a secondary rather than a primary cause.

The debate centred on the variations that were essential to evolution. If evolution were 'guided by a Higher power', it would mean, as Lyell claimed, that variations are 'the effects of an unknown law, ordained & guided . . . by an intelligent cause on a preconceived & definite plan'.[198]

Darwin had problems with this. Quite apart from anything else, it didn't really help to explain anything. 'The view that each variation has been providentially arranged seems to me to make natural selection entirely superfluous, & indeed takes [the] whole case of [the] appearance of new species out of the range of science,' he reasoned.[199] Such immediate divine 'guidance' wasn't deemed necessary in other scientific explanations. Why was evolution any different?

> Why should you or I speak of variation as having been ordained & guided more than does an astronomer in discussing the fall of a meteoric stone? He would simply say that it was drawn to our earth by the attraction of gravity, having been displaced in its course by the action of some quite unknown laws. – Would you have him say that its fall at some particular place & time was 'ordained & guided without doubt by an intelligent cause on a preconceived & definite plan'? Would you not call this theological pedantry or display?[200]

Deeming natural selection as needing to be guided, step by step, variation by variation, by an intelligent cause, effectively undid the whole theory, and put science back in the realm of special creation. 'Gray's notion of the course of variation having been led, like a stream of water by Gravity, seems to me to smash the whole affair,' Darwin remarked to Lyell. 'It reminds me of a Spaniard whom I told I was trying to make out how the Cordillera were formed; & he answered me that it was useless for "God made them".'[201]

Rejecting such an argument did not entail rejecting God, of course. 'It may be said that God foresaw how they would be made,' Darwin immediately acknowledged. But establishing an effective process whose outcomes you could 'foresee' was different from guiding that process, one single, infinitesimal variation at a time.[202]

It wasn't only that such hands-on divine guidance proved bad science, however. What did it actually mean to say that variations had been 'ordained & guided . . . by an intelligent cause'? Did that mean *every* variation, no matter how small and seemingly insignificant?[203]

'Will you honestly tell me,' Darwin asked Lyell quite seriously, 'whether you believe that the shape of my nose (eheu) was "ordained & guided by an intelligent cause"?'[204] If the answer was 'no', why should anything else be 'ordained & guided'? Why should one detail, like a swift's wing be 'ordained' and another, such as Darwin's nose, not?

If, alternatively, the answer was 'yes', all sorts of problems emerged. Any such 'intelligent cause', who needed to guide evolution every step along the way, looked not so much like God as a bad engineer. 'It seems preposterous that a maker of Universes should care about the crop of a Pigeon solely to please men's silly fancies.'[205] It reduced him to the kind of meddler in details that was more characteristic of special creation and from which evolution had rescued him.

More seriously, it implicated him in all sorts of affairs, from the tiny: 'Do you believe that when a swallow snaps up a gnat that God designed that that particular swallow should snap up that particular gnat at that particular instant?'[206] to the tragic: 'An innocent & good man stands under [a] tree & is killed by [a] flash of lightning. Do you believe (& I really should like to hear) that God designedly killed this man? Many or most persons do believe this; I can't & don't.'[207] 'The man & the gnat', Darwin reasoned, 'are in [the] same predicament.' 'If the death of neither man or gnat are designed, I see no good reason to believe that their first birth or production should be necessarily designed.'[208]

Ultimately, the debate hinged not so much on biology as theology – specifically, what concept of God one held and how far it was credible. Does God preordain? Can he foresee? What do his omnipotence and omniscience entail? These were not questions that Darwin felt comfortable with.

'Do you consider that the successive variations in size of the crop of the Pouter Pigeon, which man has accumulated to please his caprice, have been due to "the creative & sustaining powers of Brahma",' he asked Lyell in April 1860, referring to an expression that Lyell seems to have used during a visit to Downe the previous month. 'In the sense that an omnipotent & omniscient Deity must order & know everything, this must be admitted; yet in honest truth I can hardly admit it.'[209]

If God's omniscience and omnipotence meant that he pre-determined every single detail of existence no matter how tiny or unjust – every gnat caught in flight, every innocent man killed by lightning – Darwin was not persuaded. Such a concept of God had no explanatory power (indeed, it actually *diminished* the explanatory power of his theory), verged into moral culpability and appeared positively demeaning to the one who flung stars into space. In short, it was neither appealing nor credible.

If God's omniscience and omnipotence did not mean this, however, what did it actually entail? Could God foresee but not determine? If so, what relationship, if any, did he have with creation? Such questions were not limited to Darwin's correspondence with Gray and Lyell. He raised them, and indeed cited the same examples, with other friends, as he informed Gray:

> Hensleigh Wedgwood . . . is a very strong Theist, & I put it to him, whether he thought that each time a fly was snapped up by a swallow, its death was designed; & he admitted he did not believe so, only that God ordered general laws & left the result to what may be so far called chance, that there was no design in the death of each individual Fly.[210]

Darwin seemed to agree, though didn't sound very sure about it.

> I can see no reason, why a man, or other animal, may not have been aboriginally produced by other laws; & that all these laws may have been expressly designed by an omniscient Creator, who foresaw every future event & consequence. But the more I think the more bewildered I become.[211]

He was aware that he was venturing ever further into the metaphysical quagmire that he had carefully avoided all his life.

> I do not wish to say that God did not foresee everything which would ensue; but here comes very nearly the same sort of wretched embroglio as between free-will & preordained necessity.[212]

Ultimately, as he said in his autobiography, Darwin 'deserve[d] to be called a Theist' during this period. This was not because of Gray's or Lyell's arguments about how God led and guided the process of natural selection. He respected their arguments and believed sincerely that it was possible to combine their religious and evolutionary convictions. But he did not share them. Hensleigh Wedgwood's vision of a God that set the rules of the game of life and then allowed the players space to play freely within it, growing and changing as they did, seemed credible. But it did not *add* much for Darwin or, for that matter, do enough to obviate the problem of suffering. As far as he was concerned, his theory of natural selection did not exclude God but did not require him either.

His fullest, and to all intents and purposes final word on the issue came in the conclusion of his book, *The Variation of Animals and Plants under Domestication*, published in 1868. This concluding discussion was clearly the fruit of his epistolary debates with Gray and Lyell.

Natural selection, Darwin suggested, is like an edifice built at the foot of a precipice that uses for its natural materials only those 'fragments of stone' that happen to have fallen there. Although each has ended up there through natural, law-governed processes, 'in regard to the use to which the fragments may be put, their shape may be strictly said to be accidental'. But this presents us with 'a great difficulty':

> An omniscient Creator must have foreseen every consequence which results from the laws imposed by Him. But can it be reasonably maintained that the Creator intentionally ordered, if we use the words in any ordinary sense, that certain fragments of rock should assume certain shapes so that the builder might erect his edifice?[213]

The obvious answer is 'no'. We cannot assume that every fragment we find at the base of the cliff was put there by the creator just so that the edifice may be constructed. As with rock fragments, so with variations:

> If the various laws which have determined the shape of each fragment were not predetermined for the builder's sake, can it with any greater probability be maintained that He specially ordained for the sake of the breeder each of the innumerable variations in our domestic animals and plants?[214]

The illustrations he drew on would have been familiar to Gray and Lyell.

> Did He ordain that the crop and tail-feathers of the pigeon should vary in order that the fancier might make his grotesque pouter and fantail breeds? Did He cause the frame and mental qualities of the dog to vary in order that a breed might be formed of indomitable ferocity, with jaws fitted to pin down the bull for man's brutal sport?[215]

If we can't assume that such variations were ordained by this creator – and Darwin clearly implies that we can't – why should we assume that others were?

> If we give up the principle in one case, – if we do not admit that the variations of the primeval dog were intentionally guided in order that the greyhound . . . might be formed, – no shadow of reason can be assigned for the belief that [any] variations . . . were intentionally and specially guided.[216]

At this point, Darwin directly refers to Gray, secure in the knowledge that their friendship could stand the criticism.

> However much we may wish it, we can hardly follow Professor Asa Gray in his belief 'that variation has been led along certain beneficial lines,' like a stream 'along definite and useful lines of irrigation.' If we assume that each particular variation was from the beginning of all time preordained, the plasticity of organisation, which leads to . . . natural selection or survival of the fittest, must appear to us superfluous laws of nature. On the other hand, an omnipotent and omniscient Creator ordains everything and foresees everything.[217]

Put simply, as far as Darwin was concerned, you couldn't ascribe some variations to God's guidance and not others. God's role had to be either all or nothing, and since all was demonstrably absurd, it had to be nothing. It wasn't that God didn't exist. It was that, as far as natural selection was concerned, he didn't have anything to do.

Darwin was frank in these concluding paragraphs, as he had been in his correspondence with Gray and Lyell, that the issue was ultimately beyond his comprehension. He introduced the discussion in *The Variation of Animals* by saying, 'I am aware that I am travelling beyond my proper province,' and concluded it (and the book) with a similar sentiment: 'Thus we are brought face to face with a difficulty as insoluble as is that of free will and predestination.'[218]

Such self-effacement was typical but also sincere. He genuinely did feel confronted by a question that was beyond his capacity to resolve to his satisfaction. 'In truth I am myself quite conscious that my mind is in [a] simple muddle about "designed laws" & "undesigned" consequences,' he wrote to Gray, signing himself 'Your *muddled* & affectionate friend'.[219]

The result of this was that his theory directed him towards agnosticism with a distinct, if mild, atheistic flavour. Natural selection did not kill God but it did render him superfluous. But natural selection was not the whole picture.

'The universe is not the result of chance'

Darwin was alert to the fact that evolution by natural selection played out on a much larger stage. Frequently in his discussions with Gray, Lyell and others he emphasizes that although his theory does not point him in the direction of God, the universe in which it occurs does. It was almost as if Darwin felt that the play of life no longer needed a playwright because the characters were actually improvising their lines, but that everything else – the stage, the theatre, the very idea of drama itself – did require some original and creative artist.

This remained a constant theme over the last 20 years of his life. 'I see no necessity in the belief that the eye was expressly designed,' he wrote to Gray in May 1860. Having said that, 'I cannot . . . be contented to view this wonderful universe & especially the nature of man, & to conclude that everything is the result of brute force.'[220] He struck a similar note two months later. 'I cannot persuade myself that electricity acts, that the tree grows, that man aspires to loftiest conceptions all from blind, brute force.'[221]

The following year he wrote to Sir John Herschel, thanking him for a signed copy of a book in which he had mentioned Darwin and *The Origin*. Darwin had long admired Herschel, an astronomer, mathematician, chemist and philosopher who was by now the elder statesman of British science. Darwin claimed, in his autobiography, that Herschel's *Introduction to the Study of Natural Philosophy* was one of the two books that had most influenced him as a young man (the other being Alexander von Humboldt's *Personal Narrative*), and he had visited him on the last leg of his *Beagle* voyage.

He was therefore, not surprisingly, very keen for Herschel to approve of his theory and somewhat dispirited when he learnt that he had referred to it as the 'law of higgledy-piggelty'. Despite this, Darwin remained an admirer and took the opportunity of the letter to engage with one of the issues

Herschel had raised. Once again he reveals his dilemma. Natural selection points him one way, the broader framework points him another. 'The point which you raise on intelligent Design has perplexed me beyond measure,' he began.

> One cannot look at this Universe with all living productions & man without believing that all has been intelligently designed; yet when I look to each individual organism, I can see no evidence of this. For, I am not prepared to admit that God designed the feathers in the tail of the rock-pigeon to vary in a highly peculiar manner in order that man might select such variations & make a Fan-tail; & if this be not admitted . . . then I cannot see design in the variations of structure in animals in a state of nature.[222]

It was the same problem: the big picture suggested design, the little ones didn't.

> The mind refuses to look at this universe, being what it is, without having been designed; yet, where one would most expect design, viz. in the structure of a sentient being, the more I think on the subject, the less I can see proof of design.[223]

'I am driven to two opposite conclusions,' he admitted to Henry Acland, Regius professor of medicine at Oxford, a few years later.[224]

It was a tension he lived with for many years. 'My theology is a simple muddle: I cannot look at the Universe as the result of blind chance, yet I can see no evidence of beneficent Design,' he told Joseph Hooker in 1870.[225]

A year before he died, Darwin wrote to William Graham, a philosopher who was shortly to be made professor of jurisprudence and political economy at Belfast. He had recently read Graham's book *Creed of Science* and, unusually, was writing cold to thank him for it. 'It is a very long time since any other book has interested me so much,' Darwin wrote. Much as he liked the book, however, he did not agree with everything Graham had to say. For the last time in his life (he died nine months later) Darwin outlined his 'muddled' opinions on the matter of design.

> There are some points in your book which I cannot digest. The chief one is that the existence of so-called natural laws implies purpose. I cannot see this . . . [assuming] the laws as we now know them . . . the law of gravitation . . . of the conservation of energy, of the atomic theory, &c. &c. hold good, . . . I cannot see that there is then necessarily any purpose [to them].[226]

Having said that, he went on to tell Graham, 'nevertheless you have expressed my inward conviction, though far more vividly and clearly than I could have done, that the Universe is not the result of chance'.

This was the ambiguous and irresolvable tension that he took to his grave. Over the last 20 years of his life, Darwin's opinions fluctuated, although, as he told John Fordyce, 'in my most extreme fluctuations I have never been an atheist in the sense of denying the existence of a God'.[227] The fluctuation was between a theory that inclined him towards deism and atheism and a perception of the universe that inclined him towards theism. Neither sentiment carried him all the way, however, and as he grew older he became happier with the term 'agnostic'. The word not only reflected the genuine sense of not knowing, of being honestly confused, about the existence of God, but it also captured one other consideration that had crept powerfully into his thinking in his last years.

The agnostic mind of a monkey

Immediately after telling Graham that his 'inward conviction' was 'that the Universe is not the result of chance', Darwin introduced a caveat.

> But then with me the horrid doubt always arises whether the convictions of man's mind, which has been developed from the mind of the lower animals, are of any value or at

all trustworthy. Would any one trust in the convictions of a monkey's mind, if there are any convictions in such a mind?[228]

This was a concern that can be traced right the way back to his notebook speculations over 40 years earlier, but had grown in the years since the publication of *The Origin of Species*.

Darwin's correspondence with Gray in the early 1860s frequently ends with him claiming to be in a muddle. Sometimes, however, that subjective claim slipped into a more objective one. Perhaps it wasn't Darwin who was in a muddle. Perhaps the whole question was actually insoluble. Perhaps it was simply beyond human capabilities. 'I feel most deeply that the whole subject is too profound for the human intellect,' he told Gray. 'A dog might as well speculate on the mind of Newton.'[229]

Typically for Darwin, the example of a dog was not simply rhetorical. Humans were related to dogs, albeit very distantly. If you couldn't trust a dog's mind, why trust a human's? More precisely, and less outrageously, how can you know that an ape's mind is selected to detect truth?

Darwin makes this point in his autobiography, in the specific context of his religious beliefs. He explains how he was impressed by 'The extreme difficulty or rather impossibility of conceiving this immense and wonderful universe, including man with his capacity of looking far backwards and far into futurity, as the result of blind chance or necessity.'[230] This was the argument from cosmic as opposed to biological design that sustained his fluctuating theism for the last 20 years. 'When thus reflecting I feel compelled to look to a First Cause having an intelligent mind in some degree analogous to that of man; and I deserve to be called a Theist.'[231] But then came the monkey puzzle:

> Can the mind of man, which has, as I fully believe, been developed from a mind as low as that possessed by the lowest animal, be trusted when it draws such grand conclusions? May

not these be the result of the connection between cause and effect which strikes us as a necessary one, but probably depends merely on inherited experience?[232]

Moreover, the education system in Victorian Britain was set up and operated by the Church, effecting a 'constant inculcation in a belief in God on the minds of children'. Might this not produce 'so strong and perhaps an inherited effect on their brains not yet fully developed, that it would be as difficult for them to throw off their belief in God, as for a monkey to throw off its instinctive fear and hatred of a snake'?[233]

'The strongest argument for the existence of God,' Darwin told the journalist and devout Calvinist, James Grant, at the time he was writing and revising his autobiography, 'is the instinct or intuition which we all (as I suppose) feel that there must have been an intelligent beginner of the Universe. But then comes the doubt and difficulty whether such intuitions are trustworthy.'[234]

In short, could you trust your own mind? Darwin simply did not know.

Such considerations nudged him from perplexed theism to full-scale agnosticism. Darwin could not make up his mind. He genuinely did not know and did not know whether one could know. Time and again, this heartfelt uncertainty emerges in the last years of his life.

'The safest conclusion seems to be that the whole subject is beyond the scope of man's intellect,' he wrote to the Dutch writer Nicolaas Dirk Doedes in April 1873.[235] 'I am forced to leave the problem insoluble,' he told James Grant five years later.[236] 'I think that generally (& more and more so as I grow older) but not always, that an agnostic would be the most correct description of my state of mind,' he confided to John Fordyce, the following year.[237]

Such was the conclusion he reached and left to stand in his autobiography.

I cannot pretend to throw the least light on such abstruse problems. The mystery of the beginning of all things is insoluble by us; and I for one must be content to remain an Agnostic.[238]

Conclusion

The traditional picture of Darwin's religious journey is from Christianity through theism and deism to agnosticism. It is, to a large extent, accurate, although in need of some clarification. Darwin was a particular *sort* of Christian before and on the *Beagle*: civilized and Paleyian, with a faith based more on the expectations of his social class and upbringing, and on the evidence of natural theology, than on any deep scriptural convictions or personal experience.

His subsequent loss of faith was not smooth. It had begun, silently and subtly on the *Beagle* but went through some particularly disturbing rapids in the years after his return, and again a decade and a half later. This was when he encountered biblical criticism for the first time, disavowed the doctrine of eternal damnation, found himself unable to believe in miracles, witnessed the natural theological foundations of his faith being washed away, and exposed the happy world of William Paley as, at best, a mendacious half-truth. And it was also when he experienced, brutally, at first hand, the reality of natural selection. Charles and Emma Darwin had ten children. Three died young and most of the others suffered from ill-health. This wasn't the direct consequence of some historically locatable Fall. It was simply the way things were. Having held the hand of his favourite child in the last, degrading week of her short life, he was never able to reconcile what he saw about him with the benevolent, loving God of the Christian story.

Such an experience didn't extinguish his belief – faith would be too strong a word – in the existence of God, and the remaining years of his life were spent wrestling with the implications of his theory and with science in general on the subject. He could not share the conviction of some of his closest friends that God somehow guided evolution, in a hands-on, variation-by-variation kind of way. But nor could he believe that the universe and its laws were simply chance. Such a tension resulted in a fluctuating theism for many years, but Darwin was always nervous about placing too much weight on the argument from cosmological design. William Paley had done just that, 70 years earlier, in the biological field, and look what had happened.

And in any case, could he even trust his own mind over such matters? If humans were evolved from earlier primates, and Darwin had no doubt they were, their brains would have been selected for survival rather than for true belief. The capacity to acquire such beliefs may, of course, have aided survival and therefore been selected for. But who could say? Could there not be survival benefits in certain untruths? Darwin did not know, and could never decide whether it was possible to know. He remained, as he told most of those with whom he corresponded on the matter, confused and muddled. He was content to remain an agnostic.

The interesting thing was that that agnosticism was never deemed a serious loss to him. Ironically, given the number of crises of faith for which he was indirectly responsible, Darwin never had a crisis of faith himself. Religious experience had never been part of his background and he did 'not think that the religious sentiment was ever strongly developed in me'. He had needed his sister's encouragement to read the Bible even during his 'orthodox' years, and he never felt 'inwardly moved by the Holy Spirit', even when training to become a priest. He told Emma before they married that he felt that religious beliefs should make little difference to 'how one ought to act'. 'I felt no distress' when disbelief 'crept over me', he admitted in his autobiography.[239]

Overall, there is a powerful sense that the loss of his religious faith made precious little difference to him. The idea is supported by the shape of his life after 1842. Darwin had once trained to be an Anglican minister, where he would live in a country parsonage, work for his parishioners and spend as much time as possible studying nature. In 1842 he and Emma moved to Downe in Kent, where he lived in a former country parsonage. He served as the treasurer of Downe's Coal and Clothing Club, which helped provide both for the needy in the village. He proposed an investment scheme that would raise funds for the village poor, and when it was set up as the Downe Friendly Society he administered its funds. He was a member of the parish council and regularly contributed to the village Sunday School. He had his children christened at Downe church and he often gave generously towards its repairs. Later in life he accepted an invitation to be an honorary member of the South American Missionary Society, to which he made small donations. He oversaw a former schoolroom in the parish, in which his family set up a temperance reading room. When James Fegan, a local evangelist, requested use of the room in 1880 to bring his tent revival meetings indoors, Darwin not only granted permission but told him, 'Your services have done more for the village in a few months than all our efforts for many years . . . Through your services I do not know that there is a drunkard left in the village.'[240] And, of course, he spent long hours studying nature. As his friend Brodie Innes, the vicar of Downe, later remarked, 'in all parish matters he was an active assistant; in matters connected with the schools, charities and other businesses, his liberal contribution was ever ready'.[241] All in all, the pattern of his life bore an uncanny resemblance to that of a comfortable, liberal, rural Anglican clergyman.

None of this obviates the fact that he once had firm theological convictions that over the years disappeared, sometimes suddenly, sometimes gradually. Darwin did lose his Christian faith. But because of the kind of Christian he had been, the type of man he was, and the sort of society in which he lived, that loss made rather less difference to him that it might have done.

Postscript: agnostic but not apathetic

It is worth emphasizing, if only as a postscript to the story of Darwin's loss of faith, that agnostic did not mean apathetic. Darwin may have felt muddled about the whole question of God's existence and role, but he was clear about some religious issues, in particular the appropriate relationship between science and religion.

Darwin had no stomach (literally, it seems) for conflict of any kind, and he dreaded the scandal that the publication of *The Origin of Species* would create. Evolution had long been synonymous with radicalism and atheism. A book defending it, no matter how sober and well-researched, was bound to provoke a storm of protest and outrage. He remembered well the reaction to Robert Chamber's *Vestiges of Creation*, 15 years earlier.

As a result he left the fight for public approval in the hands of a few close friends, in particular Gray, Lyell, Huxley and Hooker. Some, like Gray, were Christians who promoted the theory through dialogue and accommodation with religious believers, whereas others, like Huxley, were anti-clerical agnostics who liked nothing more than to get into big battles with religious opponents.

As often as not, however, these battles were not simply about evolution. Indeed, for some of Darwin's inner circle, evolution was merely the *casus belli*, the justification for starting a war they believed was long overdue, against a religious establishment that had too much say over the composition, content and direction of British science. As Huxley wrote in the *Westminster Review* in 1860, in terms that may sound strangely familiar to modern readers:

> Who shall number the patient and earnest seekers after truth, from the days of Galileo until now, whose lives have been embittered and their good name blasted by the mistaken zeal of Bibliolaters? . . . Extinguished theologians lie about the cradle

of every science as the strangled snakes beside that of Hercules; and history records that whenever science and orthodoxy have been fairly opposed, the latter has been forced to retire from the lists, bleeding and crushed if not annihilated; scotched, if not slain.[242]

Such was the background to the most famous of such evolutionary battles, the 1860 Oxford meeting of the British Association for the Advancement of Science. This was a week-long affair but it is remembered only for a single debate in the Oxford Natural History Museum, on 30 June.[243]

According to the best-known version of the story – numerous versions were in circulation within hours of the event and to this day no one really knows exactly what was said – Samuel Wilberforce, the Bishop of Oxford, and a prominent opponent of natural selection, baited Darwin's aptly nicknamed 'Bulldog', Thomas Huxley, by asking him whether he was descended from an ape on his grandfather's or grandmother's side. 'The Lord hath delivered him into mine hands,' Huxley is supposed to have whispered, before standing up and replying that he would rather have an ape for a grandfather than a man who used his considerable gifts merely to ridicule a serious scientific discussion.

Whatever Huxley actually replied, 'the effect was tremendous'. One lady fainted and had to be carried out, dozens of people jumped out of their seats, hundreds more cheered and the event passed into history, and then legend.

In reality, the debate was only superficially about evolution. Beneath the surface there lay questions about who controlled, spoke for and directed British science. As John Hedley Brooke has written, 'the collision between Wilberforce and Huxley ... [was] a collision not so much between science and religion ... as between two different styles of science'.[244] Darwin's theory was caught up in, and to a large extent catalysed, the transition of science from being an amateur pastime of gifted Anglican clergy that was coloured with presuppositions based on natural theology, to the specialized activity of professional scientists with no confessional or, indeed, theological loyalties. For all that William Paley inspired and influenced him, this was a transition Darwin favoured. He was absent from the notorious Oxford debate just as he was for all the post-*Origin* battles. Absence did not denote disapproval, however. On the contrary, he was delighted with and wholly supportive of his pugnacious disciples. 'From all that I hear from several quarters, it seems that Oxford did the subject great good,' he congratulated Huxley. 'It is of enormous importance in showing the world that a few first-rate men are not afraid of expressing their opinion.'[245]

How was it that Darwin, fluctuating between theism and agnosticism, deeply respectful of others' religious beliefs, and ever eager to avoid controversy, could be so positive about the noisy belligerence of some of his followers?

The answer, like the Oxford debate, is only superficially about natural selection. Darwin was, of course, keen to see his theory promoted and accepted. But he was also keen to see the science that he had dedicated his life to stand as an independent and autonomous discipline.

Downe was his harbour from the storm, although it did not protect him from every wave of hostile opinion. He read reviews and often received letters from those who took issue with his life's work.

'If you were to read a little pamphlet which I received a couple of days ago by a clergyman,' he wrote to Brodie Innes, once Downe's vicar had left the parish, 'you would laugh & admit that I had some excuse for bitterness; after abusing me for 2 or 3 pages in language sufficiently plain & emphatic to have satisfied any reasonable man, he sums up by saying that he has vainly searched the English language to find terms to express his contempt of me & all Darwinians.'[246]

Darwin took such criticism calmly but it reinforced his opinion that science should be free from clerical policing.

When his once eager and brilliant Catholic disciple, St George Jackson Mivart, first fell away from natural selection on religious grounds (albeit constantly provoked by Huxley's venomous anti-Catholicism) and then became Darwin's most vigorous (and perceptive) critic, it merely reinforced his beliefs. Scientific activity and religious convictions needed to be held at arm's length. It wasn't that the one *necessarily* corrupted the other. Asa Gray, Charles Lyell and many of Darwin's other ordained scientific friends proved otherwise. It was simply that to do either justice, science and religion needed to be treated as separate disciplines.

This was the source of his frustration at having introduced the 'Pentateuchal terms' into later editions of *The Origin*. Such terms blurred the boundary between the disciplines, and Darwin, as he wrote to the manufacturer George Maw in 1861, thought 'it [was] a pity to mingle science & religion' in this way.[247]

'I thank . . . & honour you for [your judgement] that theology & science should each run its own course,' he told the mathematician Mary Boole in 1866, adding that 'in the present case I am not responsible if their meeting point should still be far off'.[248]

Most directly, three years before his death, he told the Russian diplomat Nicolai Mengden that he believed that 'science has nothing to do with Christ'.[249] In historical terms, this was about as wide of the mark as it is possible to get. Science in Britain had its roots firmly embedded in Christian belief. The founders of the Royal Society had been deeply devout men, spurred on to scientific work by their specifically Christian convictions that creation was ordered, rational and comprehensible, and that by studying it they would better understand and glorify God. Science in Britain had everything to do with Christ, at least initially.

Whether Darwin was aware of this or not, the fact was he was living not in the seventeenth century, when Christianity had first energized science, but in the nineteenth, when it was often frustrating it. For every Charles Kingsley or Frederick Temple, there were many Christians who denounced evolution on *religious* rather than *scientific* grounds – men like the anonymous clergyman who had written to Darwin vilifying him, or Robert FitzRoy, who stood up at the Oxford meeting and implored the assembled crowd to believe God's holy word rather than that of a mere human on the questions of creation. Frustrating as such denunciations were, Darwin was sure they would not win through. Referring to one such attack he remarked:

> Dr Pusey's attack will be as powerless to retard by a day the belief in evolution as were the virulent attacks made by divines fifty years ago against Geology, & the still older ones of the Catholic church against Galileo, for the public is wise enough always to follow scientific men when they agree on any subject.[250]

As far as Darwin was concerned, what was good for science was also good for theology. If science was to be respected as a legitimate discipline in its own right, so should theology. This did not, of course, mean that the phenomenon of religion should be beyond scientific examination. Darwin gave considerable space in *The Descent of Man* to analysing the 'feeling of religious devotion'.

It was more that theological enquiry should be not regulated, still less bullied, by the scientific authorities or, indeed, any others. He took some pride in the fact that this was the path he had adopted – 'I [cannot] remember that I have ever published a word directly against religion or the clergy,' he wrote to Brodie Innes, and he advised others to do likewise. 'Why should you be so aggressive? Is anything gained by trying to force these new ideas upon the mass of mankind?' he asked the atheist Edward Aveling pointedly.[251]

The same went for ecclesiastical authorities. Darwin's aversion to controversy extended beyond scientific debates, to include religious and political ones. He did, however, make one exception in the case of religion.

Shortly after *The Origin* was published, an even more controversial book hit the shops. *Essays and Reviews* was the work of seven Anglican scholars – the 'Seven against Christ' as they were nicknamed – that offered to the public a manifesto for a more liberal and broadminded understanding of the Christian faith. The essays were thoughtful, nuanced and scandalous to the orthodox.

Benjamin Jowett argued that the Bible needed to be studied in the same spirit as any other ancient text. Frederick Temple engaged positively with German higher criticism. Baden Powell (grandfather of the scout master) spoke about God as a lawgiver and openly doubted miracles. Charles Goodwin re-evaluated Genesis in the light of geology.

The authors were not revolutionaries. Baden Powell, for example, was professor of geometry at Oxford; Jowett, master of Balliol College and Regius professor of Greek; Temple, headmaster of Rugby and later Archbishop of Canterbury. But their status made the problem worse. If such educated, respectable, establishment men could cast doubts over the literal, infallible and inerrant Word of God, what might others do? Not surprisingly, the authorities were deeply unhappy, formally reprimanding the authors and defrocking two of them.

Darwin clearly felt strongly about this infringement of intellectual activity and, uncharacteristically, was prepared to show his feelings in public. He signed a public letter expressing his 'surprise and regret' that the Archbishop of Canterbury and other bishops had censured the book.

> Without committing ourselves to the conclusions arrived at in the various Essays, we wish to express our sense of the value which is to be attached to enquiries conducted in a spirit so earnest and reverential, and our belief that such enquiries must tend to elicit truth, and to foster a spirit of sound religion. Feeling as we do that the discoveries in science, and the general progress of thought, have necessitated some modifications of the views generally held on theological matters, we welcome

these attempts to establish teaching on a firmer and broader
foundation.[252]

Darwin's response to *Essays and Reviews* was his only excursion into public on a theological topic, but it clearly reflected an ongoing, rather than a one-off, concern. A few years later John William Colenso, a missionary bishop in Natal, South Africa, wrote a book re-evaluating the first six books of the Bible. *The Pentateuch and Book of Joshua critically examined* argued, in the manner of *Essays and Reviews*, that these books were and should be treated as ancient documents, but went further, claiming that they had accumulated errors and misreadings over the years. Again the authorities were outraged. Colenso was found guilty of erroneous teaching at an ecclesiastical trial in Cape Town in 1863 and was given four months to retract or be deposed from office. He petitioned the Queen to reconsider the verdict and she referred the question to the Judicial Committee of the Privy Council. Colenso's case attracted many sympathizers and soon a 'declaration in favour of freedom of opinion & defending [his] rights' was circulating. Erasmus wrote to his brother saying that he 'had no doubt whatever you would sign [it]'.[253] Neither the declaration nor Darwin's signature have been found, but it is known that Darwin contributed (the significant sum of) £5/5s to one of the many subscription funds that were established to pay for Colenso's defence. Darwin valued intellectual freedom, in whatever discipline, highly.

It was this that lay behind a bizarre exchange Darwin had with the office of the then Archbishop of Canterbury, Archibald Campbell Tait, not long before he died. In December 1880, Darwin was invited to attend a private conference at Lambeth Palace the following January, intended to 'investigate fully the real relations between Religion and modern Science', with the objective of achieving reconciliation between the two.[254]

Darwin's friendship with Lyell, Gray and others, not least his efforts to publish Gray's pamphlet 'Natural Selection not Inconsistent with Natural Theology', show that this was an objective with which he had some sympathy. However, he refused. His official excuse was his poor health but he also admitted that 'I can see no prospect of any benefit arising from the proposed conference.'[255]

Walter Browne, his correspondent on the matter, replied saying that the Archbishop was 'anxious to obtain expressions of opinion, even from those who do not see the desirability of holding such a meeting', and asking whether Darwin 'could kindly make any remarks either on particular points, or on the subject in general'.[256] Darwin responded immediately:

> I regret that it would be impossible for me to explain the causes of my disbelief in any good being derived from the conference, without treating the subject at inordinate length. I will only add that in my opinion, a man who wishes to form a judgment on this subject, must weigh the evidence for himself; & he ought not to be influenced by being told that a considerable number of scientific men can reconcile the results of science with revealed or natural religion, whilst others cannot do so.[257]

Darwin was brought up in a tradition in which science was almost a branch of theology. In the past that had served science well, but as the nineteenth century progressed and scientific discoveries – first geological, then biological – began to cast doubts on the theological orthodoxies that had birthed the discipline, serious tensions emerged.

They came to a head with Darwin's own theory. Although himself agnostic at the end of life, and sympathetic and respectful towards the religious beliefs of others, he was convinced that his life's work, and the practice of science more generally, needed to stand on its own merits. Science, like theology, needed to be respected as a legitimate, independent discipline, without unhelpful mingling.

In as far as they are fighting *this* battle, today's public atheists are indeed Darwin's legitimate disciples. But in the country of Darwin's birth at least, this battle for scientific legitimacy, autonomy and respect was won decades ago. Darwin would have been delighted.

4

What we can learn

⸻ ◆ ⸻

Darwin is a modern icon. The nineteenth century saw other scientists make discoveries that revolutionized their disciplines and remain relevant today – people like Michael Faraday or James Clerk Maxwell – but none can match Darwin's hold over the popular imagination.

And not just the popular imagination. Modern biologists still read and discuss Darwin's work, returning to it for provocation and inspiration. Darwin is regularly claimed by opposing factions to legitimate their positions. 'Darwinian' has become an epithet that biologists war over. Not even Einstein, the only comparably iconic modern scientist, can claim that.

The reasons for this are many. Darwin had unparalleled powers of observation, analysis, speculation and patience. His method was supremely thoughtful, careful and tactful. He himself was genuinely likeable.

Perhaps most significantly, however, was that he revolutionized humanity's perception of itself, challenging orthodoxies that were, in truth, already fraying at the edges. It is here that his own religious journey fits. Darwin did not claim to be a serious religious thinker. Indeed, he repeatedly insisted that the issues were beyond his capabilities and that they left him terribly muddled. And yet his loss of faith still has a great deal to teach us, as much because of its muddled and hesitant nature as in spite of it.

Superficially, it is obvious what these lessons are. His own account in his autobiography invites discussion of some

113

well-trodden areas, such as scriptural reliability (How should we read Genesis 1—3? How far can we trust divergent Gospel narratives?) and philosophical credibility (Can we believe in miracles?).

However, quite apart from the fact that it is questionable how far these issues really did destroy his Christian faith (this book has argued that other considerations loomed rather larger), any such discussion would be rather generic, less about Darwin, who wrote almost nothing on such topics, and more about general apologetic questions that fill volumes the world over.

A more interesting and more profitable avenue would be to explore what Darwin's *entire* religious journey – from the 'sort of Christian' he was in his pre-theory days, through the intellectual and personal struggles of his middle years, to the muddled and hesitant fluctuations of old age – has to teach us about faith, specifically Christian faith, today.

The faith Darwin lost

Darwin's Christian faith, up to and including his *Beagle* days, was orthodox, but orthodox in a particular, early nineteenth-century, socially secure, Anglican kind of way. Personal experience of the Holy Spirit was peripheral. Scripture played a role but primarily as a source of raw material for arguments that proved Christian truths. Reason, particularly reason based on the natural world, was paramount. Darwin's was a Christian faith based more on rational defences of the logic and coherence of the Apostles' Creed or the Thirty-nine Articles than it was a personal commitment to or moving experience of Jesus Christ. There was little space for John Wesley's 'heart strangely warmed'.

In this, he was simply an inheritor of over a hundred years of theological tradition, in which the shift to natural philosophy that had occurred in the mid-seventeenth century gradually began to edge aside the more distinctively Christian justifications for Christian faith. True, there were other 'sorts' of Christianity active in Britain at the time, even within the established Church. British Christianity had long been a broad church. But Darwin had not grown up with or into any of these. His Christianity was true primarily because the natural world pointed to structure, harmony and happiness. It was no surprise, therefore, that when he first recognized that the natural world was not as ordered, purposive or benign as had been thought, the Christian structure that towered about these foundations toppled.

There is a valuable lesson in this today, not least because several recent scientific ideas have tempted the resurrection of the kind of natural theology from which Darwin emerged, even to the extent that the respected Australian physicist Paul Davies has written 'science offers a surer path to God than religion'.[258]

The most famous of these ideas is what is known as the anthropic principle. This is founded on the recognition that not only did the universe come into existence at some point in the past (rather than having existed eternally as was believed until the 1960s) but that the mathematical constants that underpin the universe are fine-tuned to an almost inconceivable degree. Detune them even slightly and the universe would collapse in on itself, or heavier atoms would not form, or stars would burn out too quickly, or the universe would be sterile in some other way. Either way, there would be no earth, no life and no humans.

Another less well-known but equally important idea would have been particularly close to Darwin's heart. Darwin thought that evolution by natural selection removed all direction and purpose from the natural world. Things exist the way they do not because they are designed or intended but simply because they fit into a particular, temporary environmental niche. There is no purpose to life, beyond fraught attempts simply to survive.

Recent years, however, have recognized the ubiquity of convergence, 'the recurrent tendency of biological organisation to arrive at the same "solution" to a particular need'.[259] Eyes (both camera and compound), wings, legs, claws, teeth, brains, tool-use, agriculture and much else besides have evolved time and time and time again. There are, after all, only so many ways of feeding, fighting, fleeing and reproducing. 'The evolutionary routes are many, but the destinations are limited.'[260]

This has given rise to talk of the 'deep structure' of evolution. Because the physical and environmental constraints upon evolution on earth are so tight, the emergence of certain features and activities could be said to be inevitable. Rewind and replay the tape of life and you would get a picture that was strangely similar to the one we have today, one in which organisms flew, crawled, heard, smelt, watched and perhaps even walked, talked, thought and loved. Perhaps evolution does have a purpose and direction to it after all?

Not surprisingly, this was a phenomenon that Darwin himself noticed. Towards the end of his *Beagle* voyage, when in Australia, he found himself 'reflecting on the strange character of the animals of this country as compared with the rest of the world'. 'An unbeliever in every thing beyond his own reason might exclaim, "Two distinct Creators must have been at work; their object, however, has been the same, and certainly the end in each case is complete."' While musing on this he noticed a 'lion-ant' capture its prey by means of a 'hollow conical pitfall'.

> First a fly fell down the treacherous slope and immediately disappeared; then came a large but unwary ant; its struggles to escape being very violent . . . curious little jets of sand . . . were promptly directed against the expected victim. But the ant enjoyed a better fate than the fly, and escaped the fatal jaws which lay concealed at the base of the conical hollow.[261]

This, Darwin recognized, was precisely the method used by a different European species. 'Now what would the disbeliever say to this?' he wrote rhetorically in his diary. 'Would any two workmen ever hit on so beautiful, so simple & yet so artificial a contrivance? It cannot be thought so. – The one hand has surely worked throughout the universe.'[262]

Ironically, given Darwin's own Paleyian response to this example of convergence, such examples were sometimes used by detractors to criticize natural selection. St George Jackson Mivart, Darwin's admirer turned antagonist, argued in the Catholic periodical the *Month*, that the close resemblance between Australian marsupial 'wolves' and European wolves, or the similarity between the eyes of cephalopods and vertebrates, posed awkward questions for Darwin's theory. 'To have been brought about in two independent instances by merely indefinite and minute accidental variations, is an improbability which amounts practically to impossibility.'[263]

Today, as examples of convergence mount up, the temptation is to react as Darwin did in his *Beagle* journal, rather than Mivart did 30 years later, and to see intelligence lurking somewhere behind evolution. Certainly, the idea that life invariably navigates its way towards complex 'solutions', among them the moral, rational, relational, organizational features we see in mankind, corresponds well with the Christian understanding of creation, as does the seemingly life-tailored nature of the universe, as articulated by the anthropic principle.

But Darwin's story reminds us, forcefully, that to *base* religious faith on such observations is a serious mistake, inviting collapse when the next scientific revolution comes. It is one thing to investigate such phenomena as objectively as one can, and then to explore how consonant they are with a Christian understanding of creation. It is quite another to treat them as a foundation stone for one's faith.

Today's leading natural theologians are fully alert to such temptations and highly unlikely to follow in William Paley's footsteps. But that is as much due to Charles Darwin as to anyone else.

Losing his religion

Every religious group is bound together by myths, and today's New Atheists are no different. Those myths can be true but need not be. The idea that Darwin was *really* an atheist, in spite of everything he said, is one of them. The idea that he lost his faith because of his theory is another.

As we have seen, this latter claim is, at best, only partly true. The years of intense speculation after he arrived back from the *Beagle* voyage certainly destabilized the comfortable, Paleyian Christianity of Darwin's youth. And the theory of evolution by natural selection that he formulated during and after this period certainly highlighted the problem of suffering for him in a new and problematic way. But it was his *experience* of suffering, supremely in Annie's death in 1851, that finally extinguished his faith.

To this extent, the supposedly new and groundbreaking reasons for Darwin's loss of faith were, as he himself recognized, long-established and widely recognized. At heart, it was the problem of pain. What Darwin's theory did was to reformulate that problem. It alerted people to the scale and seeming necessity of suffering, not just among humans but among all sentient creatures, for whom the justification of 'moral improvement' could not be made.

That said, suffering was not the outright deal-breaker for Darwin. His musings on the subject, in relation to natural selection, were subtle and alert us to the fact that somewhere along the line, biology turns into theology and fundamental value-judgements are involved. It is not simply the case that suffering exists, end of (God's) story. There are questions about how much ('an incalculable waste'), for what ends ('the highest good, which we can conceive') and what kind of God we envisage ('to our finite minds omnipotent and omniscient').

Today some talk about the suffering of sentient creatures as if it were a conclusive argument for the non-existence of God. Others ridicule such sentiments. 'Nature is too cruel to have been invented by God! A wet, mawkish, bunny-hugging argument,' as one *Times* commentator put it.[264] Whichever conclusion one adopts, the questions we face – whether the suffering involved in natural selection is worth the good that results and whether that balance of suffering and good is compatible with our concept of God – remain judgement calls, open for each of us to answer as we see fit.

For Darwin the balance may have weighed in favour of happiness over suffering, but that was not enough. Once he had lived through Annie's wretched death, he could not reconcile the reality of suffering (albeit outweighed by happiness in the final, overall reckoning) with his understanding of God.

Given the nature of the Paleyian Christianity with which he grew up, that decision should not surprise us. Paley's 'happy world' had little room for suffering, which offended its sense of order and harmony, and it offered no resources for dealing with suffering. That was one of the reasons why Cardinal Newman railed so fiercely against it, claiming that it 'cannot ... tell us one word about Christianity proper'.

Such Christianity was more philosophical than theological, built on the foundation of seemingly secure and universal human reason rather than on the particularities of the Christian story, let alone the counter-intuitive scandal of the incarnation and the cross. Put bluntly, as soon as Christianity moved away from the foot of the cross and lost sight of the crucified God, it became defenceless against accusations of suffering and injustice. No amount of philosophical justification or arguments for the immortality of soul is enough. The pain, the sense of injustice, the sense of loss becomes overwhelming. Christianity stands by the cross or it doesn't stand at all.

In truth, Darwin's theology never stood anywhere near the foot of the cross, even during his orthodox years. The Church and the theology into which he grew never prepared or equipped him for suffering. To be sure, a loss like the one he experienced at Easter 1851 could crush any kind of religious faith, but a largely Christ-less Christianity, of a secure, happy, natural order, offered no defence at all.

Doubts that remained

Darwin died doubting whether it was even possible to trust one's own mind in questions of metaphysics. This ended up being the firmest foundation, as it were, of his agnosticism. Not only did he not know, but he didn't know whether it was possible to know.

The question remains a live one today. If it is true that the human brain, like the rest of the body, has been selected throughout its evolutionary history in order to improve the organism's ability to survive and reproduce, why should we assume it has reliable cognitive faculties? In the words of the American philosopher, Alvin Plantinga, 'Evolution is interested (so to speak) only in adaptive behaviour, not in true belief. Natural selection doesn't care what you believe; it is interested only in how you behave.'[265] In as far as true belief enables successful behaviour, meaning behaviour that helps the organism survive and reproduce, that true belief would be selected for. But who knows how far that is?

If this is so – and it is a big 'if': the debate is a live one – Darwin was right to doubt his mental ability to determine metaphysical truths but should have gone even further, doubting his mental ability to navigate physical as well as metaphysical disciplines. He never did. Indeed, it is interesting to note the restricted way he did deploy this scepticism. There were some 'instincts' he was prepared to trust and others he was not. He once told his lifelong friend John Henslow that:

> I believe there exists, & I feel within me, an instinct for truth, or knowledge or discovery, of something [the] same nature as the instinct of virtue, & that our having such an instinct is reason enough for scientific researches without any practical results ever ensuing from them.[266]

This 'instinct', a kind of sixth sense for detecting truth, was deemed trustworthy, and helped power his awesome scientific achievements. Other instincts, such as the experience of the sublime or the 'inward conviction' of God's existence, were not. It was not that Darwin did not have such instincts or experiences. When he first explored the Brazilian rainforest in April 1832 he noted in his diary, 'Twiners entwining twiners, – tresses like hair, – beautiful lepidoptera, – silence – hosannah . . . Sublime devotion the prevalent feeling.'[267] The experience made a deep impression on him and he recalled the moment in his autobiography years later.

> In my Journal I wrote that whilst standing in the midst of the grandeur of a Brazilian forest, 'it is not possible to give an adequate idea of the higher feelings of wonder, admiration, and devotion which fill and elevate the mind.' I well remember my conviction that there is more in man than the mere breath of his body.[268]

Yet that conviction was never deemed as trustworthy as the corresponding 'instinct for truth'. As Emma recognized very early on in their marriage, because that to which such 'convictions' pointed could never be proved, those convictions were deemed somehow illegitimate.

> May not the habit in scientific pursuits of believing nothing till it is proved, influence your mind too much in other things which cannot be proved in the same way, & which if true are likely to be above our comprehension.[269]

It was to prove a prescient observation. As Darwin later commented in his autobiography:

> The state of mind which grand scenes formerly excited in me, and which was intimately connected with a belief in God, did not essentially differ from that which is often called the sense of sublimity; and however difficult it may be to explain the genesis of this sense, it can hardly be advanced as an argument for the existence of God, any more than the powerful though vague and similar feelings excited by music.[270]

Darwin's sensitivity to the sublime withered as he grew older, a fact he commented on and lamented. 'Up to the age of thirty,' he wrote in his autobiography, 'poetry of many kinds, such as the works of Milton, Gray, Byron, Wordsworth, Coleridge, and Shelley, gave me great pleasure.' Nor was it just literature. 'Formerly pictures gave me considerable, and music very great delight.' But since then everything had changed.

> I cannot endure to read a line of poetry: I have tried lately to read Shakespeare, and found it so intolerably dull that it nauseated me. I have also almost lost any taste for pictures or music. – Music generally sets me thinking too energetically on what I have been at work on, instead of giving me pleasure. I retain some taste for fine scenery, but it does not cause me the exquisite delight which it formerly did.[271]

'I should like to hear [the Messiah] again,' he told Joseph Hooker in 1868, 'but I dare say I should find my soul too dried up to appreciate it as in old days.'[272] Charles has 'no poet's corner in his heart', Thomas Huxley's wife once commented.[273]

Cardinal Newman once remarked that 'Any one study ... exclusively pursued, deadens in the mind the interest, nay the perception, of any other.'[274] That certainly seemed to be the case for Darwin.

> My mind seems to have become a kind of machine for grinding general laws out of large collections of facts, but why this should have caused the atrophy of that part of the brain alone, on which the higher tastes depend, I cannot conceive.[275]

The idea that reliable truth could be communicated through such instincts, intuitions or experiences, as well as through the patient interrogation of tangible evidence, was something Darwin could never really accept. He acknowledged its possibility, telling his young disciple George Romanes in 1878 that 'reason may not be the only instrument for ascertaining [Theism's] truth.'[276] But he never deemed it seriously trustworthy.

'I cannot put much or any faith in the so-called intuitions of the human mind,' he wrote to Charles Lyell in 1874.[277]

Such scepticism may have contributed to the slow wilting of his aesthetic sensibilities. It certainly helped alienate him further from the possibility of religious faith. If, as Emma once wrote to him, 'it is feeling & not reasoning that drives one to prayer', it was clear that Darwin could never pray.[278]

Conclusion

The reasons for Darwin's loss of faith are interesting and relevant to believers and non-believers today. Questions over what constitutes legitimate and sufficient evidence for religious beliefs, or how one understands and accommodates suffering within a religious, or indeed an irreligious framework are unlikely to disappear in the near future. Darwin's 'muddled' but penetrating engagement with such questions remains of great value.

Much the same could be said for the *way* in which he engaged with those questions, indeed for the way in which he conducted himself throughout his life.

Darwin was a diligent collector and a meticulous observer, but he also recognized the need for speculation. 'I am a firm believer, that without speculation there is no good & original observation,' he wrote to Alfred Wallace.[279] He managed to combine a fierce commitment to his life's work with a genuine and disarming openness about its weaknesses. *The Origin of Species* contained an entire chapter dedicated to difficulties with the theory, which began:

> Long before having arrived at this part of my work, a crowd of difficulties will have occurred to the reader. Some of them are so grave that to this day I can never reflect on them without being staggered.[280]

But perhaps most tellingly, in spite of his loss of faith and the pain he suffered in seeing three of his children die young, he remained as courteous and respectful to those who retained religious beliefs as he was to fellow agnostics. 'I hardly see how religion & science can be kept . . . distinct,' he commented to Brodie Innes, 'but . . . there is no reason why the disciples of either school should attack each other with bitterness.'[281]

Sometimes he wondered whether he had been *too* careful. 'I may . . . have been unduly biased by the pain which it would give some members of my family, if I aided in any way direct attacks on religion,' he told the atheist Edward Aveling in 1880.[282] But he never regretted his courtesy. Family members, colleagues, friends, acquaintances, critics, even the general public honoured and respected him for it.

In an age where such courtesy and grace are notable for their absence from debates about evolution and religious belief, that is the lesson, above any other, we need to hear from Charles Darwin.

Glossary of names

Acland, Henry Wentworth (1815–1900): Regius Professor of medicine, Oxford (1858–94), Darwin correspondent

Aveling, Edward Bibbins (1851–98): atheist, socialist, Karl Marx's son-in-law, Darwin correspondent

Boole, Mary Everest (1832–1916): mathematician, teacher, Darwin correspondent

Browne, Sir Thomas (1605–82): writer on medicine, religion, science

Browne, Walter Raleigh (1842–84): founder of the Society for Psychical Research, lectured on evidences of Christianity, Darwin correspondent

Browne, William (1805–85): radically minded contemporary of Darwin's at Edinburgh

Butler, Joseph (1692–1752): bishop, theologian, philosopher, author of *The Analogy of Religion*, from which Darwin took an epigraph for *The Origin of Species*

Chambers, Robert (1802–71): Scottish author and publisher, wrote *Vestiges of the Natural History of Creation* which, controversially, put evolutionary ideas into popular hands

Colenso, Bishop John William (1814–83): first Anglican bishop of Natal, South Africa, author of the controversial book *The Pentateuch and Book of Joshua critically examined*. Darwin contributed to his legal defence fund

Comte, Auguste (1798–1857): French philosopher, positivist, wrote *Positive Philosophy*, which influenced Darwin's thinking in the late 1830s

Darwin, Anne Elizabeth (Annie) (1841–51): Darwin's first daughter and second child, died in Malvern from a 'bilious fever with typhoid character'

Darwin, Caroline Sarah (1800–88): Darwin's sister

Darwin, Charles Waring (1856–8): Darwin's youngest son and tenth child, died in infancy

Darwin, Elizabeth (1847–1926): Darwin's fourth daughter and sixth child

125

Darwin, Emily Catherine (1810–66): Darwin's younger sister

Darwin, Emma (née Wedgwood), (1808–96): Darwin's wife

Darwin, Erasmus (1731–1802): Darwin's paternal grandfather, early evolutionist, author of *Zoönomia*

Darwin, Erasmus Alvey (1804–81): Darwin's elder and only brother

Darwin, Francis (Frank) (1848–1925): Darwin's third son and seventh child

Darwin, George Howard (1845–1912): Darwin's second son and fifth child

Darwin, Henrietta Emma (1843–1930): Darwin's third daughter and fourth child

Darwin, Horace (1851–1928): Darwin's fifth son and ninth child

Darwin, Leonard (1850–1943): Darwin's fourth son and eighth child

Darwin, Mary Eleanor (b. 1843): Darwin's second daughter and third child, died at three weeks

Darwin, Robert Waring (1766–1848): Darwin's father

Darwin, Susan Elizabeth (1803–66): Darwin's sister

Darwin, Susanna (1765–1817): Darwin's mother, died when Darwin was eight

Darwin, William Erasmus (1839–1914): Darwin's first son and first child

Dirk Doedes, Nicolaas (fl. 1870s): Dutch topographical writer, Darwin correspondent

El'leparu, also known as **York Minster** (fl. 1830s): Fuegian who accompanied Darwin on *Beagle*

Fegan, James (1852–1925): nonconformist evangelist who used a room in Downe school for revival meetings, Darwin correspondent

FitzRoy, Robert (1805–65): Commander of HMS *Beagle*, 1828–36

Fordyce, John (fl. 1870s): author of works on scepticism and the modern social order, Darwin correspondent

Fox, William Darwin (1805–80): Darwin's second cousin, lifelong friend and correspondent

Goodwin, Charles (1817–78): Egyptologist, lawyer, contributor to *Essays and Reviews*

Graham, William (1839–1911): Philosopher, political economist, author of *Creed of Science*, Darwin correspondent

Grant, James (1802–79): journalist, devout Calvinist, Darwin correspondent

Grant, Robert (1793–1874): Scottish physician, early proponent of evolution, friends with Darwin in Edinburgh

Gray, Asa (1810–88): Fisher Professor of Natural History, Harvard University, 1842–88, lifelong friend and correspondent with Darwin

Gully, James (1808–83): medical doctor with a practice in Malvern who treated Darwin and his daughter, Annie

Hamond, Robert (fl. 1830s): member of *Beagle* crew

Hare, Julius (1795–1855): theological writer, edited *Remains of John Sterling*, which Darwin read in the late 1840s

Henslow, John Stevens (1796–1861): clergyman, botanist, lifelong friend and correspondent of Darwin

Herbert, John Maurice (1808–82): barrister, judge, trained for ordination with Darwin at Cambridge

Herbert, William (1778–1847): botanist, poet, clergyman, early evolutionary theorist

Herschel, Sir John (1792–1871): astronomer, mathematician, chemist, philosopher, elder statesman of British science, scientific hero of Darwin's

Holland, Sir Henry (1788–1873): physician, a Darwin cousin, whom Darwin consulted regarding his health

Hooker, Joseph (1817–1911): botanist, director of Royal Botanic Gardens in Kew, lifelong friend and correspondent of Darwin

Horner, Leonard (1785–1864): Scottish geologist, educationalist, Darwin correspondent

Humboldt, Alexander von (1769–1859): Prussian naturalist, explorer, author of *Personal Journey*, which Darwin greatly admired

Huxley, Thomas (1825–95): zoologist, friend and correspondent of Darwin, prominent defender of evolution by natural selection, popularly known as 'Darwin's bulldog'

Innes, John Brodie (1817–94): vicar of Downe, 1846–68, friend and latterly correspondent of Darwin

Jowett, Benjamin (1817–93): classicist, theologian, Master of Balliol College, Oxford, contributor to *Essays and Reviews*

Kingsley, Charles (1819–75): clergyman, professor of modern history at Cambridge, Darwin correspondent

Knox, Robert (1791–1862): Scottish surgeon, anatomist, friend of Darwin's at Edinburgh

Lamarck, Jean-Baptiste (1744–1829): French naturalist, early proponent of evolution

Lyell, Sir Charles (1797–1875): Scottish geologist, author of *Principles of Geology*, which was very influential on Darwin, lifelong friend and correspondent

Macculloch, John (1773–1835): Scottish geologist, author of *Proofs and Illustrations of the Attributes of God*

Malthus, Thomas Robert (1766–1834): economist, demographer, author of *Essay on the Principle of Population*, which was key to the formation of Darwin's theory of evolution

Matthews, Richard (fl. 1830s): missionary on board *Beagle*

Maw, George (1832–1912): geologist, botanist, tile manufacturer and Darwin correspondent

Mengden, Nicolai (fl. 1870s): Russian diplomat and Darwin correspondent

Mivart, St George Jackson (1827–1900): comparative anatomist. Initially accepted evolution but turned into one of its fiercest and most perceptive critics

Newman, Francis William (1805–97): scholar and writer, author of *History of the Hebrew Monarchy*, *Phases of Faith* and *The Soul*, each of which Darwin read around 1850, younger brother of John Henry Newman

Newman, Cardinal John Henry (1801–90): writer, theologian, author of *The Idea of a University*, convert to Roman Catholicism

Norton, Andrews (1786–1853): American preacher, theologian and author of *The Evidences of the Genuineness of the Gospels*, which Darwin read in the late 1840s

Orundellico, also known as **Jemmy Button** (fl. 1830s): Fuegian who accompanied Darwin on *Beagle*

Owen, Fanny (fl. 1830s): friend and neighbour of Darwin before the *Beagle* voyage

Owen, Richard (1804–92): comparative anatomist, prime mover in establishing the Natural History Museum, Darwin correspondent and fierce critic of evolution

Paley, the Revd William (1743–1805): theologian, Archdeacon of Carlyle, author of *Evidences of Christianity*, *Natural Theology* and *Principles of Moral and Political Philosophy*, hugely influential in Britain and on Darwin

Powell, the Revd Baden (1796–1860): mathematician, liberal theologian, contributor to *Essays and Reviews*

Pusey, Edward Bouverie (1800–82): priest, Regius Professor of Hebrew at Oxford, leading member of Oxford Movement, critic of evolution

Ridley, Henry Nicholas (1855–1956): botanist, Darwin correspondent

Romanes, George (1848–94): zoologist, close follower of Darwin

Saint-Hilaire, Étienne Geoffroy (1772–1844): French naturalist, early proponent of evolution

Sedgwick, the Revd Adam (1785–1873): geologist, clergyman, Woodwardian Professor of geology at Cambridge, 1818–73, teacher, friend and lifelong correspondent of Darwin, critic of evolution

Sterling, John (1806–44): author whose biography Darwin read in the late 1840s

Stokes, Pringle (d. 1828): first captain of *Beagle*, committed suicide

Sumner, John Bird (1780–1862): theologian, author, influential on Darwin in 1820s, Archbishop of Canterbury 1848–62

Tait, Archibald Campbell (1811–82): Archbishop of Canterbury 1868–82, invited Darwin to contribute to debate on religion and science

Temple, Frederick (1821–1902): theologian, author, contributor to *Essays and Reviews*, Archbishop of Canterbury 1896–1902, early accepter of evolution

Tristram, the Revd Henry Baker (1822–1906): clergyman, biblical scholar, ornithologist, early acceptor of evolution, subsequently turned against it

Ussher, James (1581–1656): Anglican Archbishop of Armagh and Primate of All Ireland, famously calculated earth to have been created on 23 October 4004 BC

Wallace, Alfred Russel (1823–1913): naturalist, collector, Darwin correspondent, co-author of theory of evolution by natural selection

Wedgwood, Frances (Fanny) (1806–32): Emma Darwin's sister

Wedgwood, Hensleigh (1803–91): philologist, barrister, Emma Darwin's brother

Wedgwood, Josiah (1730–95): Darwin's maternal grandfather

Whewell, William (1794–1866): mathematician, historian and philosopher of science, influential on Darwin

Wilberforce, Samuel (1805–73): theologian, Bishop of Oxford, opponent of evolution, debated Thomas Huxley in famous 1860 Oxford debate, popularly known as 'Soapy Sam'

Yokcushlu, also known as **Fuegia Basket** (fl. 1830s): Fuegian who accompanied Darwin on *Beagle*

Notes

Unless otherwise stated, letters cited below can be found at <www.darwinproject.ac.uk>. Darwin's major publications are widely available but these, as well as his less famous ones, his autobiography, his notebooks and the early drafts of his 'species sketch' are available at <www.darwin-online.org.uk>.

1   Letter to John Fordyce, 7 May 1879.
2   Edward Aveling, *The Religious Views of Charles Darwin* (London: Freethought Publishing Company, 1883), p. 5.
3   Richard Dawkins, *The Selfish Gene* (Oxford: OUP, 1976; 2nd edn 1989), p. 267.
4   John Hedley Brooke, 'Darwin and Victorian Christianity', in Jonathan Hodge and Gregory Radick (eds), *The Cambridge Companion to Darwin* (Cambridge: CUP, 2003).
5   Letter to J. B. Innes, 27 November 1878.
6   Charles Darwin, *The Origin of Species* (London: John Murray, 1859; 3rd edn 1861), p. xiii.
7   Thomas Browne, *Religio Medici* (London: 1643; Oxford: Benediction Classics, 2007).
8   Michael J. Buckley, *At the Origins of Modern Atheism* (Yale: Yale University Press, 1987), p. 39.
9   William Paley, *Natural Theology* (Oxford: OUP, 2006).
10 See Adrian Desmond and James Moore, *Darwin* (London: Penguin, 1992).
11 Erasmus Darwin, *The Temple of Nature or, The Origin of Society* (London: 1803).
12 Charles Darwin, *The Autobiography of Charles Darwin 1809–1882* (London: Collins, 1958; repr. Penguin, 2002), p. 49.
13 Darwin, *Autobiography*, p. 96.
14 Darwin, *Autobiography*, p. 22.
15 Darwin, *Autobiography*, p. 28.
16 Darwin, *Autobiography*, pp. 42–3.
17 Janet Browne, *Charles Darwin: Voyaging, Volume 1 of a Biography* (London: Jonathan Cape, 1995), p. 53.
18 Darwin, *Autobiography*, p. 48.
19 See Desmond and Moore, *Darwin*, pp. 21–44.

[20] Caroline Darwin to Charles Darwin, 22 March 1826.

[21] Letter to Caroline Darwin, 8 April 1826.

[22] Caroline Darwin to Charles Darwin, 11 April 1826.

[23] Darwin, *Autobiography*, p. 91.

[24] Darwin, *Autobiography*, p. 57.

[25] Browne, *Voyaging*, pp. 153–6.

[26] Desmond and Moore, *Darwin*, p. 47.

[27] Desmond and Moore, *Darwin*, p. 48.

[28] Darwin, *Autobiography*, pp. 56–7.

[29] Darwin, *Autobiography*, pp. 56–7.

[30] John Pearson, *Exposition of the Creed* (London: 1659).

[31] John Bird Sumner, *The Evidence of Christianity derived from its Nature and Reception* (London: 1821), p. v.

[32] Sumner, *Evidence*, p. iii.

[33] Sumner, *Evidence*, pp. 418–19.

[34] Darwin, *Autobiography*, p. 57.

[35] Desmond and Moore, *Darwin*, p. 50.

[36] John Stuart Mill, 'Whewell on Moral Philosophy', in John Stuart Mill and Jeremy Bentham, *Utilitarianism and Other Essays* (London: Penguin, 1987), p. 229.

[37] Darwin, *Autobiography*, p. 59.

[38] Darwin, *Autobiography*, p. 59.

[39] Henry Chadwick, *The Victorian Church: Volume 1, 1829–1859* (London: A & C Black, 1966), p. 527.

[40] Desmond and Moore, *Darwin*, p. 85.

[41] Paley, *Natural Theology*, p. 456.

[42] *Sermon 60: The General Deliverance*, I.6, in John Wesley, *Sermons on Several Occasions*, Pt 2, 1825 (repr. Whitefish, MT: Kessinger, 2003), p. 52.

[43] John Henry Newman, *The Idea of a University* (London: Longmans, 1907), pp. 450–1.

[44] William Paley, *View of the Evidences of Christianity* (London: 1794).

[45] Quoted in Desmond and Moore, *Darwin*, p. 66.

[46] Letter to William Fox, 23 April 1829.

[47] Browne, *Voyaging*, p. 63.

[48] Letter to William Fox, 7 April 1831.

[49] Darwin, *Autobiography*, p. 85.

[50] Charles Darwin, *Beagle Diary*, 1 July 1832.

[51] Letters to John Stevens Henslow, 18 May and 16 June 1832.

[52] Darwin, *Beagle Diary*, 7 September 1833.

[53] Charles Darwin, *Voyage of the Beagle* (London: Henry Colburn, 1839), p. 490.

54 Darwin, *Voyage*, p. 490.
55 Darwin, *Voyage*, p. 493.
56 Darwin, *Voyage*, pp. 493–4.
57 Darwin, *Voyage*, p. 607.
58 Darwin, *Voyage*, p. 499.
59 Darwin, *Voyage*, p. 512.
60 Darwin, *Voyage*, p. 500.
61 Browne, *Voyaging*, p. 330.
62 Robert FitzRoy and Charles Darwin, 'A letter, containing remarks on the moral state of Tahiti, New Zealand, etc.', *South African Christian Recorder*, September 1836, pp. 221–38.
63 Darwin, *Autobiography*, p. 101.
64 Letter to William Fox, 9–12 August 1835.
65 Letter to Leonard Horner, 29 August 1844.
66 Darwin, *Autobiography*, p. 77.
67 Darwin, *Autobiography*, p. 100.
68 Quoted in Browne, *Voyaging*, p. 137.
69 Darwin, *Autobiography*, p. 65.
70 Quoted in Browne, *Voyaging*, p. 130.
71 Browne, *Voyaging*, p. 189.
72 Browne, *Voyaging*, p. 324.
73 Darwin, *Voyage*, p. 356.
74 Robert FitzRoy, *Narrative of the surveying voyages of His Majesty's Ships Adventure and Beagle* (London: Henry Colburn, 1839), p. 378.
75 Darwin, *Voyage*, p. 370.
76 Darwin, *Voyage*, p. 370.
77 Darwin, *Voyage*, p. 369.
78 Darwin, *Voyage*, 2nd edn, p. 208.
79 Darwin, *Voyage*, 2nd edn, p. 207.
80 Darwin, *Voyage*, 2nd edn, p. 207.
81 FitzRoy, *Narrative*, pp. 148–9.
82 Darwin, *Voyage*, 2nd edn, p. 214.
83 Darwin, *Voyage*, 2nd edn, pp. 214–15.
84 Darwin, *Voyage*, 2nd edn, p. 215.
85 Charles Darwin, *The Descent of Man, and Selection in Relation to Sex* (London: John Murray, 1871), Vol. 1, p. 65.
86 Darwin, *Autobiography*, p. 90.
87 Darwin, *Voyage*, 2nd edn, p. 218.
88 Letter to William Fox, 23 May 1833.
89 Darwin, *Beagle Diary*, 19 January 1833.
90 Darwin, *Beagle Diary*, 6 February 1833.
91 Darwin, *Beagle Diary*, 6 February 1833.

[92] Browne, *Voyaging*, p. 250.
[93] Browne, *Voyaging*, p. 326.
[94] Darwin, *Voyage*, p. 320.
[95] Darwin, *Beagle Diary*, 4 November 1832.
[96] Darwin, *Voyage*, p. 320.
[97] Darwin, *Autobiography*, p. 57.
[98] H. E. Litchfield (ed.), *Emma Darwin: A century of family letters, 1792–1896* (London: John Murray, 1915), Vol. 1, p. 250.
[99] Darwin, *Autobiography*, p. 95.
[100] Litchfield, *Emma Darwin*, Vol. 2, p. 6.
[101] Emma Wedgwood to Charles Darwin, 21–2 November 1838.
[102] Emma Wedgwood to Charles Darwin, 23 January 1839.
[103] Emma Darwin to Charles Darwin, c. February 1839.
[104] Darwin, *Autobiography*, pp. 85–96.
[105] Browne, *Voyaging*, p. xi.
[106] See letter to Leonard Horner, 20 March 1861.
[107] 'Easter Day. Naples, 1849', in A. L. P. Norrington (ed.), *The Poems of Arthur Hugh Clough* (Oxford: Clarendon Press, 1968), pp. 54–8.
[108] Darwin, *Autobiography*, p. 139.
[109] Emma Darwin to Charles Darwin, c. February 1839.
[110] This section draws extensively on these notebooks, specifically B, C, D and E (on the 'transmutation of species') and M and N (on metaphysics, morals and 'speculations on expression'). These are all available at <www.darwin-online.org.uk>.
[111] Letter to Charles Lyell, 1 August 1861.
[112] Charles Kingsley to Charles Darwin, 18 November 1859.
[113] Letter to Susan Darwin, 1 April 1838.
[114] Desmond and Moore, *Darwin*, p. 249.
[115] Thomas Robert Malthus, *An Essay on the Principle of Population* (Oxford: Oxford World Classics, 1999), ch. 1.
[116] Malthus, *Population*, ch. 1.
[117] Malthus, *Population*, ch. 1.
[118] Malthus, *Population*, ch. 1.
[119] Notebook E.
[120] Sir John Sebright, *Observations upon the Instinct of Animals* (London: 1836).
[121] Letter to Joseph Hooker, 13 July 1856.
[122] Darwin, *Origin*, p. 75.
[123] Aveling, *Religious Views*, p. 5.
[124] Francis Darwin (ed.), *The foundations of The Origin of Species. Two essays written in 1842 and 1844* (Cambridge: CUP, 1909), p. 51.
[125] Darwin, *Foundations of the Origin*, p. 51.

126 Darwin, *Foundations of the Origin*, p. 52.
127 Darwin, *Foundations of the Origin*, p. 52.
128 Darwin, *Foundations of the Origin*, p. 51.
129 Darwin, *Foundations of the Origin*, p. 52 (emphases added).
130 It should be noted that I follow here the conventional explanation for the delay in publishing *The Origin*, i.e. that Darwin was nervous about publishing a scientific theory that would be associated with and give legitimacy to political radicalism, and that he was only provoked into publication by Alfred Russel Wallace in 1858 (despite already having been working on a lengthy exposition of his theory for two years). More recently, John van Wyhe has argued that Darwin did not, in fact, intentionally delay publication but was simply busy analysing, writing and publishing the results of the *Beagle* voyage, while all the time constructing and testing his theory. See John van Wyhe, 'Mind the Gap: Did Darwin avoid publishing his theory for many years?', *Notes and Records of the Royal Society*, 2007, Vol. 61, pp. 177–205.
131 Quoted in Desmond and Moore, *Darwin*, p. 295.
132 Quoted in William E. Phipps, *Darwin's Religious Odyssey* (Harrisburg: Trinity International Press, 2002), p. 49.
133 Quoted in Browne, *Voyaging*, p. 468.
134 For Darwin's reading over this period see James Moore, 'Of love and death: Why Darwin "gave up Christianity"', in J. Moore (ed.), *History, Humanity and Evolution: Essays for John C. Greene* (Cambridge: CUP, 1989), pp. 212–16, on which the following paragraphs draw.
135 Emma Darwin to Mrs Hensleigh Wedgwood, 20 October 1842, quoted in Litchfield, *Emma Darwin*, Vol. 2, p. 78.
136 Emily Darwin to Charles Darwin, 13 November 1848.
137 Letter to William Fox, 27 March 1851.
138 Letter to Susan Darwin, 19 March 1849.
139 Letter to Emma Darwin, 17 April 1851.
140 Letter to Emma Darwin, 18 April 1851.
141 Letter to Emma Darwin, 18 April 1851.
142 Letter to Emma Darwin, 18 April 1851.
143 Letter to Emma Darwin, 19 April 1851.
144 Letter to Emma Darwin, 19 April 1851.
145 Emma Darwin to Charles Darwin, 19 April 1851.
146 Letter to Emma Darwin, 20 April 1851.
147 Letter to Emma Darwin, 21 April 1851.
148 Letter to Emma Darwin, 21 April 1851.
149 Quoted in Desmond and Moore, *Darwin*, p. 383.
150 Letter to Emma Darwin, 23 April 1851.

[151] Letter to William Fox, 29 April 1851.
[152] Charles Darwin's reminiscence of Anne Elizabeth Darwin, 30 April 1851.
[153] Letter to Thomas Huxley, 18 September 1860.
[154] Litchfield, *Emma Darwin*, Vol. 2, p. 137.
[155] Letter to William Fox, 8 February 1857.
[156] Letter to Alfred Russel Wallace, 1 May 1857.
[157] Letter to Charles Lyell, 18 June 1858.
[158] Letter to Charles Lyell, 18 June 1858.
[159] Letter to Charles Lyell, 25 June 1858.
[160] Letter to Joseph Hooker, 29 June 1858.
[161] Henry Ridley to Charles Darwin, between 13 and 28 November 1878. Pusey's sermon, 'Un-science, not science, adverse to faith' was, in fact, preached by Henry Parry Liddon on Pusey's behalf on 3 November 1878 in Oxford. It was then printed in the *Undergraduate's Journal* on 7 November 1878, although the annotated edition to which Henry Ridley refers was not published until at least 13 November 1878.
[162] Letter to Henry Ridley, 28 November 1878.
[163] Letter to Alfred Russel Wallace, 22 December 1857.
[164] For the reception of *The Origin*, see Janet Browne, *Charles Darwin: The Power of Place, Volume 2 of a Biography* (London: Jonathan Cape, 2003), pp. 82–125; also Janet Browne, *Darwin's* Origin of Species: *A Biography* (London: Atlantic Books, 2006).
[165] Henry Baker Tristram, 'On the Ornithology of Northern Africa', *Ibis*, 1858, Vol. 1, Issue 4, pp. 415–35.
[166] Adam Sedgwick to Charles Darwin, 24 November 1859.
[167] Letter to Charles Lyell, 3 December 1859.
[168] Charles Kingsley to Charles Darwin, 18 November 1859.
[169] Browne, *Power of Place*, p. 96.
[170] Darwin, *Origin*, p. ii.
[171] Darwin, *Origin*, 2nd edn, p. ii.
[172] Alister McGrath, *The Order of Things: Explorations in Scientific Theology* (Oxford: Blackwell, 2006), pp. 68–9.
[173] Darwin, *Origin*, pp. 185–6.
[174] Darwin, *Origin*, p. 488.
[175] Darwin, *Origin*, 2nd edn, p. 484.
[176] Darwin, *Origin*, 2nd edn, p. 490.
[177] Letter to Joseph Hooker, 29 March 1863.
[178] Letter to *Athenæum*, 18 April 1863.
[179] Letter to Asa Gray, 22 May 1860.
[180] Darwin, *Origin*, 2nd edn, p. 481.

181 Letter to John Fordyce, 7 May 1879.
182 For a good overview of the Darwin–Gray correspondence, see Michael B. Roberts, 'Darwin's Doubts about Design: the Darwin–Gray correspondence of 1860', in *Science and Christian Belief*, 1997, Vol. 9, pp. 113–27.
183 Letter to Thomas Huxley, 20 July 1860.
184 Asa Gray, *Darwiniana: Essays and Reviews Pertaining to Darwinism* (New York: 1876), p. 5.
185 Asa Gray to Charles Darwin, 10 January 1860.
186 Letter to Asa Gray, 22 May 1860.
187 Letter to Charles Lyell, 15 April 1860.
188 Letter to Asa Gray, 26 November 1860.
189 Letter to Asa Gray, 22 May 1860.
190 Darwin, *Origin*, p. 201.
191 Darwin, *Autobiography*, p. 88.
192 Darwin, *Autobiography*, p. 88.
193 Darwin, *Autobiography*, p. 89.
194 Letter to Asa Gray, 5 June 1861.
195 Letter to Asa Gray, 5 June 1861.
196 Darwin, *Autobiography*, p. 90.
197 Letter to Charles Lyell, 15 April 1860.
198 Letter to Charles Lyell, 21 August 1861.
199 Letter to Charles Lyell, 1 August 1861.
200 Letter to Charles Lyell, 21 August 1861.
201 Letter to Charles Lyell, 1 August 1861.
202 Letter to Charles Lyell, 1 August 1861.
203 Letter to Charles Lyell, 21 August 1861.
204 Letter to Charles Lyell, 21 August 1861.
205 Letter to Charles Lyell, 15 April 1860.
206 Letter to Asa Gray, 3 July 1860.
207 Letter to Asa Gray, 3 July 1860.
208 Letter to Asa Gray, 3 July 1860.
209 Letter to Charles Lyell, 15 April 1860.
210 Letter to Asa Gray, 10 September 1860.
211 Letter to Asa Gray, 22 May 1860.
212 Letter to Charles Lyell, 1 August 1861.
213 Charles Darwin, *The Variation of Animals and Plants under Domestication* (London: John Murray, 1868), Vol. 2, p. 431.
214 Darwin, *Variation*, p. 431.
215 Darwin, *Variation*, p. 431.
216 Darwin, *Variation*, p. 431.
217 Darwin, *Variation*, p. 432.

218 Darwin, *Variation*, pp. 431–2.
219 Letter to Asa Gray, 3 July 1860. Emphases in original.
220 Letter to Asa Gray, 22 May 1860.
221 Letter to Asa Gray, 3 July 1860.
222 Letter to John Herschel, 23 May 1861.
223 Letter to Frances Wedgwood, 11 July 1861.
224 Letter to Henry Acland, 8 December 1865.
225 Letter to Joseph Hooker, 12 July 1870.
226 Letter to William Graham, 3 July 1881.
227 Letter to John Fordyce, 7 May 1879.
228 Letter to William Graham, 3 July 1881.
229 Letter to Asa Gray, 22 May 1860.
230 Darwin, *Autobiography*, p. 92.
231 Darwin, *Autobiography*, p. 92.
232 Darwin, *Autobiography*, p. 93.
233 Darwin, *Autobiography*, p. 93. Interestingly, this was the one sentence in her husband's autobiography to which Emma took serious objection. She wrote to her son Frank, as he was editing the autobiography in 1885, asking him to omit it, saying:

> There is one sentence in the Autobiography which I very much wish to omit, no doubt partly because your father's opinion that all morality has grown up by evolution is painful to me; but also because where this sentence comes in, it gives one a sort of shock— and would give an opening to say, however unjustly, that he considered all spiritual beliefs no higher than hereditary aversions or likings, such as the fear of monkeys towards snakes.

She went on:

> I should wish if possible to avoid giving pain to your father's religious friends who are deeply attached to him, and I picture to myself the way that sentence would strike them, even those so liberal as Ellen Tollett and Laura, much more Admiral Sullivan, Aunt Caroline, &c., and even the old servants.

234 Letter to James Grant, 11 March 1878.
235 Letter to Nicolaas Dirk Doedes, 2 April 1873.
236 Letter to James Grant, 11 March 1878.
237 Letter to John Fordyce, 7 May 1879.
238 Darwin, *Autobiography*, p. 94.
239 Darwin, *Autobiography*, p. 87.

240 Letter to James Fegan, between December 1880 and February 1881.
241 Francis Darwin (ed.), *The Life and Letters of Charles Darwin, Including an Autobiographical Chapter* (London: John Murray, 1885), Vol. 1, p. 143.
242 Thomas Huxley, 'Darwin on *The Origin of Species*', in *Westminster Review*, 1860, Vol. 17, pp. 541–70.
243 This encounter is covered in virtually every Darwin biography and every account of the history of science and religion ever written. See, for example, Browne, *Power of Place*, pp. 118–24, and Desmond and Moore, *Darwin*, pp. 492–9. For a superb analysis of why the debate happened, see John Hedley Brooke, 'The Wilberforce–Huxley Debate: Why Did It Happen?', in *Science and Christian Belief*, 2001, Vol. 13, pp. 127–41.
244 See Brooke, 'Wilberforce–Huxley Debate'.
245 Letter to Thomas Huxley, 20 July 1860.
246 Letter to J. Brodie Innes, 27 November 1878.
247 Letter to George Maw, 13 July 1861.
248 Letter to Mary Boole, 14 December 1866.
249 Letter to Nicolai Mengden, 5 June 1879.
250 Letter to Henry Ridley, 28 November 1878.
251 Aveling, *Religious Views*, p. 5.
252 Letter to Frederick Temple, 28 February 1861.
253 Erasmus Darwin to Charles Darwin, 1 February 1864.
254 Walter Browne to Charles Darwin, 16 December 1880.
255 Letter to Walter Browne, 16–21 December 1880.
256 Walter Browne to Charles Darwin, 21 December 1880.
257 Letter to Walter Browne, 22 December 1880.
258 Paul Davies, *God and the New Physics* (Harmondsworth: Penguin, 1990), p. ix.
259 Simon Conway Morris, *Life's Solution: Inevitable Humans in a Lonely Universe* (Cambridge: CUP, 2003), p. xii.
260 Conway Morris, *Life's Solution*, p. 145.
261 Darwin, *Voyage*, p. 442.
262 Darwin, *Beagle Diary*, 19 January 1836.
263 Quoted in Browne, *Power of Place*, p. 330.
264 Libby Purves, 'Richard Dawkins, The Naïve Professor', *The Times*, 7 August 2008.
265 Alvin Plantinga, 'Naturalism Defeated', unpublished paper, 1994: available at <www.calvin.edu/academic/philosophy/virtual_library/articles/plantinga_alvin/naturalism_defeated.pdf>.
266 Letter to John Henslow, 1 April 1848.
267 Darwin, *Beagle Diary*, 17 April 1832.

268 Darwin, *Autobiography*, p. 91.
269 Letter to Caroline Darwin, *c.* February 1839.
270 Darwin, *Autobiography*, p. 91.
271 Darwin, *Autobiography*, p. 138.
272 Letter to Joseph Hooker, 17 June 1868.
273 Quoted in Browne, *Power of Place*, p. 152.
274 Newman, *Idea of a University*, p. 359.
275 Darwin, *Autobiography*, p. 139.
276 Letter to George Romanes, 5 December 1878.
277 Letter to Charles Lyell, 3 September 1874.
278 Emma Darwin to Charles Darwin, some time in June 1861.
279 Letter to Alfred Russel Wallace, 22 December 1857.
280 Darwin, *Origin*, p. 171.
281 Letter to J. B. Innes, 27 November 1878.
282 Letter to Edward Aveling, 13 October 1880.

Further reading

There is, of course, no substitute for reading Charles Darwin himself. His *Voyage of the Beagle* is probably the most readable of his published books, *The Origin of Species* (of course) the most important, and *The Descent of Man* the most obviously relevant to his religious beliefs. Readers looking for any substantial discussion of those beliefs in these books will be disappointed, however, as only his short *Autobiography* offers any extended discussion of his religion. Beyond such publications, the Darwin Correspondence Project, <www.darwinproject.ac.uk>, is a wonderful place to browse, as is the Complete Works of Charles Darwin online, <www.darwin-online.org.uk>.

At the time of writing, there were two major biographies of Darwin in print, Janet Browne's two-volume work *Voyaging* (Volume 1) and *The Power of Place* (Volume 2), and Adrian Desmond's and James Moore's older but highly readable *Darwin*. Between them these books come to nearly 2,000 pages, but they are both well worth reading. Browne's *Darwin's* Origin of Species: *A Biography* is also interesting.

As noted in the Introduction, there are only a few works dealing specifically with Darwin's religious beliefs. The only book is William Phipps' *Darwin's Religious Odyssey*, published in the USA in 2002. Beyond that, there is Frank Burch Brown's pamphlet *The Evolution of Darwin's Religious Views*, published by the National Association of Baptist Professors of Religion (Special Studies Series, Number 10) in 1986; Maurice Mandelbaum's essay 'Darwin's Religious Views' (*Journal of the History of Ideas*, Vol. 19, No. 3, June 1958); John C. Greene's 'Darwin and Religion' (*Proceedings of the American Philosophical Society*, Vol. 103, No. 5, October 1959); and an essay by James Moore entitled 'Why Darwin "gave up Christianity"', which is published in *History, Humanity and Evolution: Essays for John C. Greene* (Cambridge University Press, 1989), which Moore edited. All, unfortunately, are difficult to get hold of. John Hedley Brooke has an essay on Darwin's religious belief in the recently published *Cambridge Companion to* The Origin of Species. This was not available at the time of writing, although John Brooke did generously offer his expertise on a draft of this book.

The paucity of books specifically about Darwin and religion is made up for by the wealth of ones on Darwin more generally and on Darwinism and religion. Of the first group, the *Cambridge Companion to Darwin* is very good, as is Michael Ruse's *Charles Darwin* (in the Blackwell Great Minds series) and Tim Lewens' *Darwin* (in the Routledge Philosophers series).

Of the second group, Denis Alexander's recently published *Creation or Evolution: Do We Have to Choose?* is excellent, as is Alister McGrath's *Dawkins' God: Genes, Memes and the Meaning of Life*, Michael Ruse's *Can a Darwinian be a Christian?* and Mary Midgley's *Evolution as a Religion*. Generally speaking, anything by Alexander, McGrath, Ruse and Midgley is worth reading.

On the extent and nature of non/evolutionary beliefs in the UK today, and their perceived relationship to theism, there is a series of important studies conducted by Theos, the public theology think tank, and the Faraday Institute for Science and Religion, in partnership with several research organizations. These come under the title Rescuing Darwin and can be found at <www.theosthinktank. co.uk>.

There are also, of course, a number of superb books on evolution itself, such as almost anything by Steven Jay Gould, Steve Jones, Daniel Dennett and Richard Dawkins. Dawkins' *The Blind Watchmaker* is particularly good. More academic but extremely interesting and important is Simon Conway Morris' *Life's Solution: Inevitable Humans in a Lonely Universe* published by Cambridge University Press in 2003.

On the Darwin wars generally, Andrew Brown's book *The Darwin Wars: How Stupid Genes became Selfish Gods* is incisive and entertaining, as is John Cornwell's *Darwin's Angel*.

Finally, *Science and Christian Belief*, the bi-annual journal of Christians in Science, is a superb resource and one well worth subscribing to.

Index

Index

Creator 59, 81, 92, 93; God as xiii, 47, 48, 78, 88; omnipotent and omniscient 94; two distinct Creators 116

Darwin, Annie Elizabeth (Darwin's daughter) xiii, xiv, 58, 65; illness and death 66–71, 73–4, 118, 119
Darwin, Caroline Sarah (Darwin's sister) 5, 8–9
Darwin, Charles: Annie's illness and death 66–71, 73–4, 118, 119; awarded the Royal Medal 74; Christianity on the *Beagle* 16–23; Christianity pre-*Beagle* 10–16, 100, 114; Christ's College, Cambridge 12–16; Complete Works xii; defence of missionaries 22–3; in Downe, Kent xiv, 58, 64, 102, 105; Edinburgh University 6–7; Emma's assessment of faith 43–5; father's death 64–5; health diary 65–6; ill-health 61, 65–6; letters and notes to Emma 38–40; letters to Emma about Annie 66–7; loss of faith 31–3, 40–6, 100–2, 117–19; at Malvern 65–6; marries Emma Wedgwood 38; mother's death 63; and ordination 9–10, 15; studies medicine 6–7; therapeutic holiday to Ramsgate 66; thoughts on marriage 35–6; training as Anglican minister 102; works *see* individual titles
Darwin, Charles Waring (Darwin's son) 75
Darwin, Elizabeth (Darwin's daughter) 65, 66
Darwin, Emily Catherine (Darwin's sister) 64
Darwin, Emma (née Wedgwood, Darwin's wife) 37–40, 58, 64–6, 100, 102, 121, 123; assessment of Darwin's faith 43–5; Darwin's letters to about Annie 66–7; edits Darwin's *Autobiography* 41–2, 138 n233; letters and notes from Darwin 38–40; marries Darwin 38
Darwin, Erasmus (Darwin's grandfather) 4–5, 37; *Zoönomia* 5

Darwin, Erasmus Alvey (Darwin's brother) 5, 6, 35, 109
Darwin, Francis (Frank) (Darwin's son) 65, 138 n233
Darwin, George Howard (Darwin's son) xii, 25, 65
Darwin, Henrietta Emma (Darwin's daughter) 65, 66, 70–1
Darwin, Mary Eleanor (Darwin's daughter) 64
Darwin, Robert Waring (Darwin's father) xii, 5, 9, 37, 58, 64–5
Darwin, Susan Elizabeth (Darwin's sister) 49, 64, 66
Darwin, Susanna (Darwin's mother) 5, 63
Darwin, William Erasmus (Darwin's son) 58, 65
Darwin Correspondence Project xii
Davies, Paul 115
deism/deists xiii, 2, 3, 97, 100
Deity *see* God
Descent of Man, The (Darwin) 29, 107
design 3
Desmond, Adrian 10, 15
Devil, the 51
Dirk Doedes, Nicolaas 99
Downe, Kent xiv, 58, 64, 102, 105; Coal and Clothing Club 102; Friendly Society 102

Einstein, Albert 113
Elizabethan Poor Law 54
El'leparu *see* York Minster
English Churchman 77
epigraphs *see Origin of Species*
Essays and Reviews 108–9
eternal damnation 63, 100
evolution 8, 48–54, 58–60, 74–5, 88–94, 95–6, 103–5, 115, 118, 120; deep structure of 116; God in 46, 84–5, 101; and morality 138 n233

faith 43–5, 57
Fall, the 57, 100
Faraday, Michael 113

143

Index